DINGHY SAILING

The Skills of the Game

THE•SKILLS•OF•THE•GAME

DINGHY SAILING

Rob Andrews

The Crowood Press

First Published in 1995 by
The Crowood Press Ltd
Ramsbury, Marlborough
Wiltshire SN8 2HR

**British Library Cataloguing in Publica-
tion Data**

A catalogue record for this book is
available from the British Library.

ISBN 1 85223 901 8

Picture Credits
All photographs by Richard
Langdon/Ocean Images, except for Fig
1, which is supplied by LDC Racing Sail-
boats/KOS; Fig 4, which is supplied by
Minorca Sailing Holidays; Fig 32, which
is by Peter Bentley; and Fig 115, which
is by Concept 2 Ltd.

All line-drawings by Bob Constant.

Typeset and designed by D & N
Publishing, Ramsbury, Wiltshire.

Phototypeset by Dorwyn Ltd.

Printed and bound by Redwood Books,
Trowbridge.

Typefaces used: text, Univers 55; head-
ings, Univers 65 and Plantin.

Picture previous page: Shirley Robertson, GBR Europe representative at the
1992 Olympic games, Barcelona, Spain.
Photo by Peter Bentley.

ACKNOWLEDGEMENTS
I would like to thank everybody who
helped me in the production of this book,
in particular: sailors Paul Brotherton,
GBR 470 representative 1992 Olympics;
John Merricks, IYRU World Champion;
Ian Walker, IYRU World Champion;
Shirley Robertson, GBR Europe representative 1992 Olympics; Mark Littlejohn,
Laser National Champion; Ian Maynard,
sport psychologist. For Loan equipment,
Performance Sailcraft for the Laser 4000;
Douglas Gill for sailing clothing; Queen
Mary Sailsports for providing the perfect
central location; Concept 2 for providing
the rowing machine. For photographs I
would like to thank Richard and Marie at
Ocean Images for keeping life in perspective with their unique humour when
deadlines had passed due to the weather! Finally, thanks to Penny Way for being
herself.

Contents

At last, here we have a book which allows dinghy sailors of all abilities to grasp the techniques that the top sailors have been developing for years. The step-by-step instruction and brilliant photographs allow readers to progress at their own speed, while the boats used should suit sailors of conventional and new generation asymmetric dinghies.

The contribution of the UK's best sailors is testimony to the standard of the book and Rob's own position as one of the leading coaches.

John Merricks
IYRU World Sailing Champion 1994

Rob Andrews has grown up through the development of modern day dinghies. Since the age of four he has played on the water in a variety of craft. He has progressed through a multitude of dinghies and keelboats, eventually sailing Olympic class 470s in the ill-fated trials of 1980 when Britain did not send its sailing team to the Olympics. Since then he has attended the Olympics as a coach on three occasions in 1984, 1988 and 1992. Rob is best known as a coach; however, he has recently been sailing new designs of dinghy, finishing second in the RS400 National Championship and winning rounds of the Audi Laser 5000 Eurocup events.

Rob is the most successful UK Olympic coach at World Championship level and has helped Nigel Buckley, Pete Newlands and Penny Way to World titles in Olympic classes. He now coaches on a freelance basis and contributes to the world's yachting press, as well as lecturing at Southampton Institute.

Rob Andrews is one of the best qualified coaches in Britain to write this new book. Not only has he worked with élite competitors over the last three Olympic Games, but he also brings the balance of his grass-roots experience.

Much of this experience was gained by his obvious delight in being on the water, be that in a coach boat or sailing in a dinghy. He has recently taken to competing as well as coaching, the results showing that he has listened to his own advice.

The book itself has excellent photograph sequences, which are the next best substitute to Rob himself talking you through a manoeuvre. It also places a great emphasis on self coaching which I also believe is a key factor in an individual's enjoyment and improvement.

Rod Carr
Olympic Sailing Team Manager 1996

Introduction

Welcome to the sport of dinghy sailing. It is a sport that has given me a great deal of fun over the last thirty years or so, and provided me with my employment. It is also a sport that is now experiencing a period of change. The boats are changing, and the type of racing in which we participate is changing, as is the club structure that supports the sport. Like any period of change, it is producing conflicts and some uncertainty that will have to be resolved. What I can say is that I have never been so optimistic about the future of the sport as I am at the moment. It is armed with this optimism that I have set about creating a dinghy sailing book for the new generation.

This book will look at new techniques

Fig 1   The RS 400, one of the new generation of dinghies, designed by Phil Morrison.

that will stand you in good stead for the coming years, as well as concentrating on those techniques still being used during this evolutionary stage. I don't expect readers to start at the beginning and progress to the end, but to use the book as a form of reference that they return to again and again. The concept of the book is that it will suit a wide range of abilities; some readers will race and some readers will simply be sailing and having fun.

As I come from a coaching background, sometimes I will explain techniques that I know will work, and act very much in the role of the instructor. At other times I will move into my coaching role and try to create a supportive environment within which you can progress, as you will have to reflect on your own experiences. After all it is you who is the performer, and you will need to experience different ideas and situations, drawing your own conclusions. This environment will allow you to experience many different aspects of the sport and you will be able to draw upon that experience to make the best decisions at the correct time in your future dinghy sailing.

I have also put together the best simple thoughts and ideas from the premier dinghy sailors in Britain. Sometimes it is the simple idea that may allow you to understand a new area, or open up a whole new technique in an existing area. At the end of this project, I hope that you will be in a position to get more out of this great sport, a sport that offers more than racing, more than competing against yourself and the natural elements.

1
The Changing Sport

The mid-1990s are going to be remembered as a time when dinghy sailing experienced some major changes that would influence the sport. I believe these changes need to be recorded, so that the sport takes on a complete perspective. If you want to rush on to the next chapter, please do, knowing that a brief history of the sport is recorded here for you to return to later.

Sailing has featured in every modern-day Olympics since 1900, although it was only in the 1950s that the sport really started to grow. In the UK, two factors were very important: plywood and designer Jack Holt. Holt developed boats like the Enterprise dinghy (for the *News Chronicle*) in 1956, a two-person hard chine boat, which remains popular today and is still characterized by its blue racing sails. Prior to this, in 1947, Holt had designed a youth trainer, the Cadet, which also retains its popularity and is also of plywood.

Holt continued designing a vast array of dinghies and keelboats, and in 1962 teamed up with Barry Bucknell to design the Mirror dinghy. Like the Enterprise, this was designed for a leading newspaper, the Mirror group. The design was a breakthrough as it incorporated mass-production plywood panels with a new stitch and glue construction. The stitch and glue effect was achieved by using copper wire to hold and stitch the plywood panels together, then sealing and bonding them with strips of glassfibre tape and polyester resin. Given the simplicity of construction, the promotion of a national newspaper and the low cost of mass-production plywood panels, the boat was a success. Thousands of the red sails could be seen on reservoirs around the UK, on boats sailed by their proud builders. Sailing had just become available to the man in the street. Based on a DIY environment and launched into the new leisure era, 70,000 of the 1.4m Mirrors have since been built, making it the most popular self-build boat.

The Mirror marked the crossroads of construction technology between plywood and glassfibre. Total glassfibre construction was offering the larger builders access to this leisure market, while the customers were offered maintenance-free sailing. The prospect of dinghy sailors locked away in the garage in the winter months lavishing coats of varnish and paint on their beloved dinghies was becoming a high price to pay for the resultant leisure time. The cost of these hand-crafted dinghies had been steadily rising as befitted a product where the constructor's skill level was as high as a cabinet maker's. The glassfibre revolution affected Europe and the USA more than the UK, which probably had the highest number of dinghy classes of any country. Perhaps the British tradition for design had fostered all these easy-to-develop wooden and plywood classes. Alternatively it may be the British love of committees that allowed all these classes to be supported by voluntary committee structures.

Meanwhile, specific designs for glassfibre construction had started to appear, with boats like the 470 and 420 in Europe and the Sunfish in the USA. In the UK, designers were more concerned with converting existing plywood designs into glassfibre construction. As the plywood had predominantly been flat-panel construction, this was a retrograde step. Glassfibre construction in the 1960s only suited curved panels as technology had not advanced to the sandwich construction that in the 1980s would once again allow flat panels to be built stronger in sandwich/glass construction than in plywood. The introduction of glassfibre boats not only meant less maintenance, but also meant dinghy sailing started to enter the leisure market-place, as large manufacturers could become involved, using mass-production glassfibre manufacture.

Ian Proctor, who along with Jack Holt will be remembered as a pioneer in dinghy design, designed a dinghy called the Topper in 1976. This was originally designed for production in glassfibre, and subsequently became the world's largest injection moulding boat. In collaboration with ICI and Rolinex, moulds were produced and the 3.4m singlehander was built from durable polypropylene. Made of the same material as your washing-up bowl, this was to be the most durable dinghy and soon became popular with sailing schools and the youth market.

The 1970s also saw the development of the Laser, from the board of Canadian designer Bruce Kirby. This boat has turned into one of the most popular dinghies of all time. Since its conception in 1971, over 150,000 boats have been built in foam-sandwich glassfibre construction world-

Fig 2   The Laser 4000, a manufacturers' one-design class featuring asymmetric spinnaker, single trapeze and weight equalization through adjustable racks.

wide. The Laser is 4.23m long and is predominantly used as a singlehander, making its Olympic début in 1996. It also marked the arrival in the 1980s and 1990s of the global marketing of dinghy sailing.

The companies involved in dinghy manufacture are becoming bigger, often part of large leisure groups. They have the means to develop new products and the marketing strategies to promote them. These companies are a product of the 1990s where leisure time and the activities involved in leisure are changing. The forecast of the 1980s was for increasing leisure time. The reality is decreasing leisure time being offered to a society with more disposable money. The new leisure activities are more excitement-orientated and are just as much fun competing against your own ability as against opposition. We now push ourselves harder in search of excitement. Look at the new sports: windsurfing, jet biking, snow boarding. They are all highly enjoyable without the need to race others.

Dinghy sailing is joining this form of leisure. The new boats of the mid-1990s are great fun to sail, even when not racing. They are low-maintenance boats, made from modern materials and performance-orientated. They are invariably built by large specialist manufacturers, who recognize that you have taken up dinghy sailing to sail and enjoy the outdoors, rather than to spend the winter maintaining your boat. The new generation of boats have followed the lead of the Laser, in that they are manufacturers' 'one-designs' where all the boats are supplied by the manufacturer and all of them are identical.

This places the skill element on sailing the boat and not developing a new sail to give the speed advantage. If Jack Holt was the designer for the 1960s, then Phil Morrison is the designer who is responsible for this new generation of boats. He was behind the Laser 4000 and the RS 400, as well as playing a major part in the design of the Laser 5000.

Materials, designs and the will on the part of the manufacturers to make exciting boats have led to this 'revolution', because that is what it is. These boats will see us into the next millennium. So how different are they to the plywood and glassfibre generation boats? In terms of construction, not that much, apart from being more comfortable and more functional, and having been subjected to extensive pre-production development. Certain new materials, notably carbon fibre, will allow lighter and stronger boats to be built. The rigs are lighter with the emphasis being put on fully battened mainsails to give

more control and longer lasting sails, as they don't flap as much as conventional sails in the dinghy park. We have also seen the introduction of the asymmetric spinnaker, which will revolutionize the way we sail and the way we handle the spinnaker. I cannot say enough about how much easier this is compared to a conventional spinnaker system. Once used you will never want to go back to the old spinnaker systems. For me, a dinghy sailor for thirty-four years, this is the most significant breakthrough in having fun in a dinghy I have experienced. Sailing this new generation of boats is like rediscovering sailing, so that all the excitement that you are now experiencing in learning to sail has been rekindled in my own sailing. It is probably best described by just one word: fun!

Fig 3   Paul Brotherton.

'Dinghy sailing in the next century will be typified by exciting, fast boats with weight equalization, putting a premium on ability and not on physical size.'

Paul Brotherton, GBR 470 representative, 1992 Olympics

2
Getting Started

LEARNING TO SAIL

Sailing Schools *(Fig 4)*

As you will have read in Chapter 1, I am very impressed with the new generation of 'manufacturers' one-designs', many of which have asymmetric spinnakers. What, however, is the best way to start sailing? This book, as I state in the Introduction, will not teach you to sail, but it will give you many hints and enough advice to save you time in getting to a standard where you can enjoy the sport. The easiest way to learn to sail is to go to a recognized sailing school. These schools will teach you according to a set scheme and are officially acknowledged by the sailing federation within your country. Within the UK, the federation is called the Royal Yachting Association (RYA), who have 1,000 recognized teaching establishments around the country. The scheme is structured from levels 1–5, and many of these schools will be part of the 1,000-odd sailing clubs in the UK.

The boats used at these schools will be either singlehanders or larger, multi-person boats, like the Wayfarer. You should decide at what pace you would like to learn and how wet you like getting! The single-handed route in Toppers, Picos or Lasers with training rigs is by far the most fun for the adventurous. You are on your own, so helm *all* the time; it is you who will make all the decisions, good and bad, so the speed of learning is very fast. Your instructor will either be in a similar dinghy, so that he or she can show you manoeuvres, or will be in a rescue boat. Briefings are very important in this style of teaching as the instructor is not in the boat with you. To offset this, sessions may start on a simulator on dry land, so that you understand exactly what you will be trying to achieve. The area that you are sailing in will be carefully controlled and rescue boats will be on hand if you should make a mistake and capsize. I used this method of teaching when I worked for the Sports Council-owned National Sailing Centre, and can guarantee that it is the quickest, most enjoyable way to learn. It can be a little tiring in strong winds, with a number of capsizes, but for the adventurous is the best way to learn to sail a dinghy.

If you do not like the thought of pushing out onto the water in a boat on your own, then the boat with an instructor is the ideal way for you. At most schools in the UK the Wayfarer is used, often with three students and one instructor to each boat. It does mean that you can have demonstrations by the instructor on board and have questions answered at any stage. On the negative side, you are only helming for a third of the time of your fellow students in the single handers. For the rest of the time you will

Fig 4   Minorca Sailing Holidays' base in the sun. A very safe venue with a wide variety of boats to suit everyone, from the beginner through to the most advanced.

be sharing the crewing tasks and have plenty of time to watch the scenery go by. Towards the end of your course the instructor will leave the three of you on your own, once he or she is confident that you have enough skills to sail quite happily on your own.

Sailing schools are also recognized by the federations to operate abroad, so if you would like to take a sailing holiday (and learn your skills in a warmer climate!), then this is an option. This approach through recognized courses is just one way that you can learn to sail. It is the route that I would recommend as it is safe, structured and you know that the

school you are going to attend has met certain standards in terms of instructor-qualification and equipment as laid down by the federation. You could, of course, just buy a boat and try to teach yourself to sail. Within the UK we have no licences for our boats, so this is possible. However you will take a very long time to learn within this non-structured environment and you may be a safety risk to yourself and others.

Sailing Clubs

If you don't want to go to a sailing school, then the next best option is to contact your local sailing club. You can find out about them from the phone book or from your national federation. As I stated earlier, this may be the site of your nearest sailing school, as more and more clubs are now offering better services for their members, including instruction. Because sailing, like all sports, is now competing for your custom, the clubs have to provide services that will make you go sailing rather than take up other leisure activities, like playing squash or tennis. The club sailing schools will run on the same syllabus as a commercial school, this being the syllabus of that country's National Sailing Federation. Courses will probably be less intense and run for a longer time-period, often being at weekends or one night each week in the summer months. When I learned to sail it was often with other club members, particularly if you were very keen to crew for them in their boats. This allowed them to have a regular crew and allowed me to learn helming skills by watching them as I improved my crewing skills. I still think that this is an option, although we now have more single-handed boats where the sailor is independent. It may be worth asking about.

TYPES OF BOAT *(Fig 5)*

If you do go to your local school or club, you will also note that the types of boats used will vary considerably. As you know, I believe that the new generation of boats are easier to sail and a lot more fun. However, as they are relatively new, there are still not many available second-hand, while there are vast stocks of second-hand sailing dinghies in the marketplace. The new boats are very good value for money, but you should consider which club you want to join, and which classes of boats they sail. The choice is really only difficult when you decide to buy a two-person spinnaker boat. In the single-handed market, deciding what type of boat to buy will depend on your body weight, which club you belong to and what type of sailing you will be doing. Laser have gone some way to solving this problem by designing three different size rigs for the standard Laser hull. If you are light you will use the smaller rig and progress in rig size as your skill level increases. This strategy is very similar to that which is successfully employed in windsurfing, where again you learn on the smaller rig and progress in size.

While talking about body weight it is also worth noting that youth schemes exist in most countries, where certain boats have been identified as being ideal for youth sailors. Within the UK these classes receive extra funding from the RYA to give training for youth members. In the UK the progression for single-handers is Optimist / Topper / Laser. The pinnacle of this scheme worldwide is the World Youth Championship, where the boys compete in Lasers with full rigs and the girls, who are lighter, compete with the Laser 'M' rig. You will find the RYA scheme for youth sailing replicated the world over.

The double-handed decision is more complex, due to the variety of classes that are available and the recent introduction of the asymmetric spinnaker. Again the club where you are going to sail will have an impact on your decision as it is more fun sailing within a fleet, rather than being the odd one out in the handicap fleet, no matter how much fun your boat is to sail. You will also find that

Single Handed

Novices	Optimist/Topper	Cadet/Mirror
Intermediate	Optimist/Topper/Laser Radial	Cadet/Mirror/405
Advanced	Laser1/Laser Radial/Europe	420/Laser 2

Single-handed Classes			**Two-handed Classes**		
	Age Range	Weight Range		Age Range	Weight Range Both Crew
Laser 1	15+	70–83 (11–13)	420	15+	108–127 (17–20)
Laser Radial	15+	54–70 (8.5–11)	Laser 2	15+	121–140 (19–22)
Europe	15+	50–66 (8–10$1/2$)	405	11–16 Boys 11+ Girls	92–112 (14$1/2$–17$1/2$)
Topper	12–15	51–67 (8–10$1/2$)	Mirror	6*–15	95–113 (15–18)
Optimist	6–14	38–54 (6–8$1/2$)	Cadet	6*–15	85–105 (13$1/2$–16$1/2$)

* as crew

Fig 5 Information on suitable boats for specific age and weight ranges. Provided by the Royal Yachting Association (1993).

the boats that are popular at your club will invariably be good for the specific conditions that exist. As dinghy sailing is held on any stretch of water, from rivers and reservoirs to estuaries and the open sea, the classes sailed have to be able to cope with the predominant conditions. The new generation of asymmetric spinnaker boats will probably not perform at their best on small rivers and specific designs have evolved that are good in these conditions.

Body weight, your sailing ability and your attitude towards excitement or risk are all part of the equation. It would be stupid to recommend the Laser 5000, which is a high-performance, two-man, twin-trapeze boat, with adjustable wings and asymmetric spinnaker, to anyone who had not mastered single-trapeze high-performance sailing. At the end of the day, choosing a boat will be a highly individual decision based on the above factors, not to mention the important factor of money. You will need to be a dedicated dinghy sailor to invest the thousands of pounds required for a new generation dinghy. Dinghy sailing magazines will give you a guide to second-hand and new prices, or alternatively you can visit a boat show. In the UK we not only have London International, but many regional shows and a specialist dinghy show with nearly all the hundred-odd dinghy classes represented.

We are in a transitional stage in dinghy development, as very few schools are yet teaching on asymmetric spinnaker boats. They will argue that while the vast majority of boats are using the conventional systems, why should they teach the minority way? Dinghies do last a long time, so the last generation of boats will still be sailed for many decades to come, supported by established class associations. Meanwhile, those who have experienced the new designs will find it almost impossible to return to the old designs. It is only a matter of years before the juniors of today will have learnt to trapeze and spinnaker-reach with an asymmetric in a Hobie 405. As their body weight increases, they will progress to a single-trapeze asymmetric boat or stay in non-trapeze asymmetric boats like the RS 400. Finally they will move onto a high-performance craft such as the Laser 4000, before trying the ultimate dinghy, the Laser 5000 or 18-foot skiff. Even if our sailors move on to keel boats they will find a parallel generation of boats, designed to be fun and easy to sail, and all with asymmetric spinnakers. The Melges 24, built by British Aerospace for the European market, is the leader in this field.

The final chapter in this story will be the direction in which the Olympics progresses. The fourteen-year-old in his Hobie 405 in 1995 will be nineteen or twenty for the Sydney Olympics in the year 2000. The classes for Olympic Games have yet to be chosen, but I hope and suspect that this new generation of asymmetric high-performance boats will be represented at those Olympics. It will be for the good of dinghy sailing in the next century.

Fig 6   Melges 24, a high-performance, four-person keelboat with asymmetric spinnaker.

3
Clothing

The clothing that you will require in order to participate comfortably and safely in dinghy sailing in Northern Europe is expensive. It is not worth compromising, so first decide if you are serious about the sport and only then buy the specialist clothing. At first you may not have a problem if you are trying to learn the sport in a sailing school. Many of these schools will be able to hire a wet suit for you; you will also be starting your sailing during the warmer months. You may even be starting the sport as part of a foreign holiday, where specialist clothing may not be needed to protect you from the Northern European climate!

Fig 7   A rear-zip dry suit being closed. Note how the sailor is holding out his arms to aid the zipping. Warning! Remember to vent the dry suit of air before going afloat.

THE DRY SUIT *(Fig 7)*

Once you have decided that you want to progress in the sport, then is the time to make the decision about whether to buy a dry suit or a wet suit. They rely on opposite principles to work. The dry suit prevents all water entering the suit and the occupier wears multiple under-layers to stay warm. The suit will be wind-proof as well as waterproof. A recent innovation in this area is the front-entry design, although the rear-zip version still remains popular. As the zip is the most likely place for water entry, strong waterproof zips have been incorporated. The flexibility of these zips is limited, hence the original suit had a rear zip across the shoulders. The down side of this design is that you either need to have a friend zip you in, or have amazing flexibility to complete the task on your own!

This problem has been recognized by the manufacturers who have introduced the diagonal front zip. The advantages and disadvantages of the rear and front zip relate to the differences in movement, clothing bulk and ease of zipping. The rear-zip suit fits the shoulders as they curve forward, is generally more comfortable and interferes less with movement of the arms; it is also more comfortable when worn with a trapeze harness. The disadvantage of the front zip is that it tends to buckle, which is not very good for the zip. It also has more material at the front which flows forward when hiking. However its big advantage is that it allows self-zipping, as well as the option of slightly venting the suit when you are hot. However this should only be done on dry land. The reason for this is that should you fall in the water through an inadver-tent capsize, the suit will fill with water. This will make it impossible to climb out of the water and back into your boat!

The other safety tip with dry suits is that you must expel all air from the suit prior to going sailing. This is easily achieved by simply squatting down and doubling your body up while allowing the air to escape through a wrist seal. Alternatively, as you launch your boat, squat down in the water and release your neck seal. The pressure of the water will expel the air from your suit. Should you not perform this action, once in the water any trapped air can move around in the suit making it very hard to maintain your balance in the water. The worst scenario is that the air goes to your feet, which then want to float to the surface!

The seals are the vulnerable part of dry suits. They are made from latex rubber and will feel quite constricting at first as they rely on pressure. Because of this constricting nature, care should be taken when squeezing your wrists and neck through the seals. Your feet seals will either seal against your leg in a similar way to the wrist seals or you will have latex boots, allowing you to wear socks as part of your undergarment layer. Recent design changes have tried to incorporate protection of the seals from ultraviolet rays by the introduction of cuffs. This development, plus correct care of the garment, will result in long life.

The material body of the dry suit is also about to undergo a revolution as breathable fabrics start to be designed for the marine environment. At present, within the dry suit you are subject to a closed environment and your own sweat production. To counter this, layered clothing will wick this sweat away from the skin and maintain body temperature. Correct under-layers will make your sailing more comfortable. Choose polyester-based clothing, which wicks any moisture away from the skin, and choose multiple layers for more warmth. Avoid wearing cotton underclothing as it has very little wicking ability and will cool the skin. The present design of dry suits has slowly been evolved from early diving versions. Style and fit are becoming more important features for the fashion-conscious dinghy market. The suits will always be large-fitting to allow the variable layers to be incorporated to reflect the sailing season. However, they may be the best choice, particularly for higher-speed craft where wind chill is a factor.

THE WET SUIT *(Fig 8)*

The alternative is the wet suit, which works by trapping a very thin layer of water between your skin and the suit. Constructed from neoprene rubber, the wet suit must fit correctly to provide the warmest environment. As the internal layer of water is heated by your body, it can only cope with being a thin layer, hence the need for the correct fit. Large amounts of water in a badly fitting wet suit will not be heated as they move around and will thus not provide the insulation that you need. Flexibility is the great attribute of the wet suit, not only in body movement, but also in the construction. As the suit is constructed, different thicknesses of material can be incorporated to reflect the function of that particular area of the suit. Often you will see thicker body sections to provide greater insulation and less flexibility. The arms and legs will be thinner to allow greater movement at the expense of warmth. The surfaces of the neoprene rubber can also have material bonded to them. This may be on the inside to allow smoother and warmer entry into the suit. Material may also be bonded to the outside to give colour or greater protection against abrasive surfaces on the boats.

Recent developments have been aimed at trying to restrict entry of large quantities of water through better control at the entry points (similar to the seals on the dry suit). Zip technology has also improved to prevent water ingress through the zip. The idea is to heat a limited amount of water next to the skin, which may be part perspiration, rather than repeatedly warming larger volumes of water. Material advances have been made by laminating reflective screens into the suit to try to prevent extra heat loss. The majority of heat loss is caused by the wind evaporating water from the outside of the suit, working in exactly the same way as our skin produces sweat, so that the moisture can be evaporated away to cool the body. As we do not want to cool the body, we must prevent this. Any material bonded onto the rubber will hold water and thus aid the evaporation and cooling.

This is the dichotomy that we have with wet suits: a double-lined suit will allow ease of dressing and also be hard-wearing, but we know that the evaporation will make it slightly cooler than a single-lined one (when the lining is on the inside of the suit). The single-lined suit allows ease of dressing, and can be easily spotted by its black rubber outside. It is warmer but slightly more vulnerable to nicks in the rubber. Alternatively you can always wear a protective suit made from waterproof nylon, which also gives extra wind-proof protection.

19

Fig 8   Both sailors are wearing wet suits. The crew has opted for a dinghy smock to provide added protection from the wind and spray.

A recent innovation is to wear a dinghy smock on top of the wet suit. The smock provides an extra layer of protection for the core of the body. Constructed from PU-coated nylon, the smock gives excellent spray protection as well as flexibility. Advances in adjustable cuff design and neck design give water little opportunity to enter. Half-way to a full dry-suit top, this combination gives much greater flexibility to the conventional wet suit.

The final choice is yours, and will depend on your own warmth requirements, your type of boat and the venue where you normally sail. I prefer the wet suit as it is snug-fitting with excellent flexibility for moving around in the boat.

As most of my sailing has been done on the open sea, where you tend to be out for longer than on reservoirs, I favour the single-lined version with a smock top. This choice may mean that you have to check the boat carefully for sharp screws, abrasion points and so on to prevent the wet suit being pierced. I have also been sailing mainly high performance dinghies where you are constantly moving about the boat to maintain speed, which means the minimum of heat loss. Perhaps with the new advances in dry suits and breathable materials we may see a move away from the black rubber-clad dinghy sailors to new brighter colours in the dry suits.

SAFETY AND COMFORT
(Figs 9 & 10)

Visibility is very important from the safety aspect, and all dinghy sailors should wear buoyancy aids. These will be specified in most race instructions, but I would recommend them every time you go sailing. You do not want to rely on rescue facilities, so you should be able to swim prior to taking up dinghy sailing. The buoyancy aid will simply do what it says, that is aid your swimming, as opposed to a life-jacket, which when inflated will turn your head the right way up and support your weight. The standard buoyancy aids are constructed from closed cell foam, and should fit you well as they are available in a variety of sizes. They are designed for ease of movement and may be designed for a specific purpose, e.g. trapezing, by being cut away where a harness is worn. From July 1995 all buoyancy jackets and life-jackets sold in Europe will have to comply with common standards set by the Comités Européen de Normalisation (CEN). The CEN standard is now published as a British Standard. Four Newton standards have been introduced: but the 50-Newton jacket is the one that will be recognized as a typical dinghy buoyancy aid.

The top and bottom of your body are vital to heat loss and the subsequent enjoyment of dinghy sailing. As we lose so much heat from the top of the head, this is the first place to protect as soon as the temperature drops. Many thermal hats in a variety of styles are available from leading manufacturers. As far as footwear goes this is a vital area for protection as well as grip. French manufacturers Aigle revolutionized footwear design with a flexible short boot, complete with side lacing to allow a snug fit. In the 1990s this design

Fig 9   A close-fitting buoyancy aid with cut away at the front for use with a trapeze harness.

has been refined by many manufacturers in order to achieve greater flexibility and warmth. One of the favoured options is the wet-suit boot, made from neoprene with a side zip to allow ease of entry. The sole is important for grip, both on the cockpit floor and on the side of the boat while trapezing. The instep should also be reinforced to spread the load when hiking in the toe straps. If you have a choice between lace sides and zip sides, remember that the lace version will give you better support, so will better suit those who hike. The zip version will be slightly more flexible and suit the trapeze crew or helm.

As sheet size has been decreased in an effort to save weight, so too has the strain

21

on the hands increased. Gloves have been developed to give added protection. Made from leather or synthetic substitutes, these round off your sailing kit. The accessories you may still require are warm clothes for the layers under your dry suit, a set of hiking shorts and a trapeze harness. We will deal with the trapeze harness under the trapeze section. The hiking shorts have become particularly popular in the single-handed classes, such as the Laser. Worn in a similar way to a pair of shorts, they provide reinforcement at the back of the thighs to spread the load. In singlehanders without a trapeze, speed is often equated with work rate, so the longer you maintain maximum hiking the better. I would only recommend these for sailors who progress to national championship level.

Finally, in a number of photographs of elite-level sailors, you will see that they wear water jackets. Consisting of flexible containers of water, and worn on the upper body to increase the righting moment of the sailor in a hiking or trapezing position, these jackets have now been shown to result in injury if the sailor is not adequately fit. Eventually they will be banned by the governing body of the sport, but in the meantime I would not recommend anyone to wear them. The key to warmth and comfort is correct-fitting garments that have been properly designed for the job in hand. Take your time in buying these goods, first decide the parameters of boats, venue and commitment to the sport. Buy them from a specialist dinghy shop where they will have a wide range, allowing you to choose the correct fit. Their specialist knowledge will also help in making the correct choice from the many alternative garments.

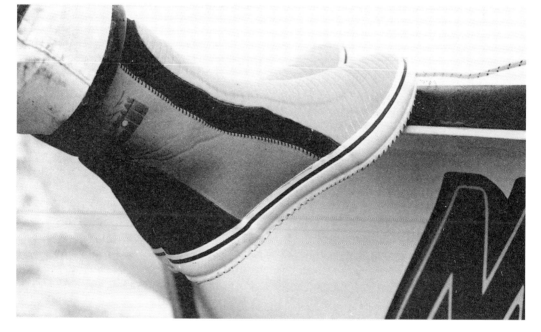

Fig 10   Boots are essential to provide the support and protection for feet. Available in lace or zip versions for different roles within the boat.

4

Goal-Setting

As a coach I think the biggest help I can give you in enjoying dinghy sailing is not by telling you how to carry out technical moves, but how to set realistic goals. I will explain techniques, but even they will be modified by your boat, yourself and individual circumstances. I hope that I will create an environment within which you can evaluate and learn. A key to creating the correct environment is to understand goals and how they affect you.

GOALS AND DREAMS

We all need dreams to help motivate or give us vision and direction for the future. The only problems with dreams are that they tend to be long-term and in some cases may not be realistic. As you take up this sport of dinghy sailing, your dream may be one day to represent your country at the Olympic Games. In a sport such as sailing where the experience factor is probably much higher than the physical factor this may be realistic, as long as you accept the commitment to learn and understand the experience factor. In other sports, where technique, fitness and age are important, the chances of going to the Olympics may be extremely remote. At the end of the day the goal of participating in the Olympics, being the pinnacle of many competitive sports, will only be attained by a small band of very

dedicated athletes. However, developing the ability and knowledge to sail around the world may be a challenge that many can aspire to. The sheer fact that we have problems identifying realistic dreams is the root of the problem. Have dreams to motivate you, but do not confuse them with realistic goals or the art of goal-setting which will structure your learning and development in the short term.

Goal setting was born within workplace psychology, where the aim was to develop systems that would create greater productivity. Sport has since developed goal-setting, which is now an accepted practice for giving performers improved direction. I want to use goal-setting to allow you to progress in dinghy sailing and have more fun. So what is a goal and how long does it last for? The first thing to say about goal-setting is that it is not magical. It is simply a way of structuring your progress in a sport by using realistic measurement, combined with feedback on your progress. For goals to work they have to be 'smart', which I will explain in more detail later. They may also consist of long-term and short-term goals. The problem with long-term goals (more than a year) is that it is very hard to decide how to achieve them, as they are so large and stretch into the future. To provide *focus* we need to break them down into smaller goals, on which we can then concentrate. Any large job is easier if broken down into smaller parts. Sailing consists of many areas that we will need to put together as a whole, e.g. tacking/gybing/hoist spinnaker/trapezing. In order to start on this learning curve we first need to learn how the boat fits together, how to launch the boat, how to sheet the sails and how to steer the boat. Our long-term dream may be to win a race at a national championship, our long-term goal may be to achieve a sailing ability that will allow us to sail competently in a force 5 wind and our short-term goal may be to learn how to assemble the boat ready for launching.

An important point is that the goal is within our control, while the dream is not. We only have control over our sailing, not control over the sailing of others. We should only judge our performance and improvements by how we perform. Do not look solely at results in races to judge your improvement. For a start, only one person wins the race, but many people within that race will have achieved a personal best. Within our sport there are no times, speeds or distances by which we can judge our performance, so people tend to use results. In other sports they have personal-best times, distances, weights, duration and so on. Have more fun: judge yourself by your own performance and not by the performance of others.

'SMART' GOALS

When deciding what your goals are it is important to ensure that they conform to the theory of 'smart' goals. On New Year's Day or Eve many people decide that the goal for the new year is to get fit. Due to the fact that this usually does not comply to the 'smart' goal theory most people fail to achieve this fitness and find themselves making the same goal the following year. It should really be called a wish as goals are designed to be achieved and give us the focus to achieve them. So what is a 'smart' goal?

Specific
Measurable
Achievable
Recordable
Time-phased

A 'smart' goal has to comply with the above criteria. To consider this let us look at my wish of getting fit this year. To start with, it is not very specific – what does fit mean? Does it mean fitter than I am now or fit enough to take part in a marathon? Both of these may mean very different standards. The last element, time-phased, has not been addressed as I haven't said by when I aim to get fit, or over what period. I haven't said how fit, so there is no chance of measuring this factor. Due to all of this vagueness the target, my fitness, is neither recordable nor achievable, and I would probably repeat the same wish the following year. It would not be achieved because I would not draw any focus, motivation or discipline from the goal.

So this year I will make a real goal, but based upon the same subject: 'I intend to train in a gym for a minimum of three days a week. I will base my training on endurance running/cycling/rowing/stepping and train for forty minutes each session. My target heart beat for this training is 65 per cent of the maximum heart rate for my age.' This goal complies with the 'smart' criteria, as it is very specific, measurable ('Did I go to the gym three times this week?'), and attainable, in relation to my work load, social life, family commitments and present level of fitness. It also specifies what I do each week, so it is time-phased. I can therefore record the details in a training log, thus complying with the recordable element. The probability is that I will stick to this goal, improving my fitness level, decreasing my fat levels and ensuring a healthier body with all the positive implications this brings. In order to decide on this goal I may have needed some specialist help – an instructor at a health club will have given me this knowledge. What he or she will not know is my personal situation, so my honest appraisal of how much time I can devote to my goal will be very important.

Having seen 'smart' goals in action, how can this be applied to sailing? The first thing to decide is what competence level you wish to achieve and by what date. You may not have started sailing or you may already be competent in a force 4 wind, but the decisions are the same: where do you want to be and by when. The goals that you create will be your guide along this route. If you have yet to take up the sport it is harder to decide where you want to go as the parameters are not yet in place. Your goal may be to join a sailing course for one week. Decide if you like the sport and then progress to your local club, deciding what dinghy to buy based upon your experiences on the course and at the club. Once you have a dinghy you may decide to go sailing once a week and have lessons at the club every three weeks. Your instructor will be able to advise you on what is a realistic rate of progress.

Later on in this book I will talk about Performance Profiles (*see* Chapter 13), which I believe individuals can use to identify strengths and weaknesses in

their sailing. These areas can also be identified by instructors or coaches, where a trained eye will save you much time struggling with a particular technique. Dinghy sailors appear still to have a resistance to using coaching. The same people would not dream of starting a sport such as golf without instruction. This resistance is slowly decreasing, as is the ability of individuals to self coach.

SELF COACHING

Mistakes or areas of weakness are often seen by many in sport as negative. I have the opposite view, believing that this identification by evaluating our performance allows us the opportunity to improve. By concentrating on our weakest area, improvement will occur. If we can combine this with concentrating on the area that will give us the biggest possible improvement on the racecourse or in enjoying our sailing we will have the largest gain. You may sail a singlehander and constantly get into 'irons' in tacking. This is spoiling your start when you race and disrupting your sailing when sailing for fun. Concentrate on this area rather than constantly practising your strongest areas, e.g. gybing.

In sailing it is also imperative that we accept responsibility if we are to improve. Dinghy sailing is one of the most open sports possible with many variables. Each day the wind varies in strength, it changes direction, or it gusts; the course changes, the length of the course varies, and we sail on rivers, lakes, estuaries or the open sea; the waves change in direction, height and speed. Consider this with the 100m sprint in athletics. This has the same track length, is always straight, and never has more than eight athletes – it also probably starts at the time stated in the programme.

Because sailing is so 'open' a sport, it is easy to avoid accepting the responsibility of the decisions that you make while sailing. Often you will hear sailors saying that the wind was all over the place and a particular competitor was lucky, forgetting that they had positioned themselves in that place by making decisions. If we fail to take responsibility for those decisions we will never improve. We will never accept that we need to get better in that area. Consider our single-handed sailor who is always in 'irons'. If he or she believes that this problem is the fault of the rudder shape, then they will never practise sufficiently to solve the problem, and will probably end up selling their boat. Only then perhaps will they discover that it is really their problem as they find themselves yet again in 'irons', but in a different type of singlehander.

> 'A comprehensive goal-setting programme should be the fundamental foundation upon which the most successful sporting preparation is based.'
>
> **Ian Maynard, British Olympic Sailing Team Sport Psychologist**

Fig 11 Olympic Laser sailing; the difference between the top sailors is probably all down to mental skills.

5
The Mainsheet System

One reason why this book concentrates on creating an environment where you learn from your own actions is that there is no one way of achieving a certain manoeuvre. If we look at the simplest dinghy, a single-hander with one sail, we soon realise that the control of this one sail can be achieved by the mainsheet attached to the end of the boom or attached to the middle, offering transom and centre mainsheeting. It would appear that this just gives us a choice; however, once we realize that this controls which way we face while tacking and gybing, the choice becomes more confusing. When describing the difference between the transom and centre mainsheet system we also have to realize that some boats have a combination. The Laser singlehander has a transom system that is then led along the boom to the front of the cockpit. We will describe this as a centre main boat as it is where the mainsheet terminates that forces us to face one way or another when tacking and gybing.

I must admit that I prefer the centre main, although many popular boats still retain the aft, transom main, the popular Topper being just one of these. The main reason that I prefer the centre main is that you always face the direction in which you are going when tacking or gybing. We will consider the tacking process by

looking at the photographs and diagrams in the next two chapters. Before considering the difference between tacking and gybing with the various mainsheet systems, it is important to understand the function of some of the sail controls.

THE MAINSHEET *(Figs 12–14)*

The mainsheet is probably the most important control, being similar to the accelerator in a car. It controls the sideways position of the boom, which is attached to the sail. Attention to detail in playing the mainsheet cannot be emphasized enough. At any level it is this attention to detail which will have the greatest affect on speed. As the boat heels we must respond and keep the dinghy upright. This can be achieved by hiking harder or going further out on the trapeze. If both of these options have been exhausted, as both helm and crew are flat out, then the mainsheet must be eased to keep the boat upright.

We will talk about pointing the boat higher if you are beating to de-power later in the book. If you do not have this option or are on a reach, then ease the mainsheet. As gusts strengthen and decrease, the mainsheet will be constantly played to

27

Fig 12   With the centre mainsheet system both hands can be used to play the mainsheet. You use your tiller hand as a cleat while your front hand repositions itself on the mainsheet.

provide the optimum power-setting. Some mainsheet systems, particularly centre main systems, will have a cleat. The angle of this cleat must be checked to allow ease of cleating combined with easy un-cleating. For downward cleating systems check that the sheet just enters the teeth of the cleat when the mainsheet is pulled across the deck at your side. This will allow you to take a rest from playing the mainsail, but also allow very easy un-cleating should a gust arrive when the mainsail is cleated. This cleat is particularly useful when hoisting spinnakers and so on, although this hoisting is increasingly becoming the domain of the crew.

Great emphasis has been given in recent years to making the centre main or transom main as efficient as possible. If we consider that its primary function is to position the boom sideways, then I think you will understand all the recent trends. Hoops, strops and adjustable strops have all been designed to have the mainsheet load transferred into the boat as high in the boat as possible. In this way we pull the boom sideways and not downwards. We want to be able to centre the boom as easily as possible. The easier this is to do, the more you will play the mainsheet, making the boat go faster.

In lighter winds we want to use the mainsheet purely to position the boom. In these winds we want a centred position (further out on a singlehander) with no down force as this affects the leech shape. In light winds we want twist in the sail as the wind speed further up the sail will be much greater than at the bottom. We will not be using the kicking strap as we do not want to affect the leech shape. Hence any mainsheet system which centres the boom while exerting as little down force as possible will be ideal. The idea of

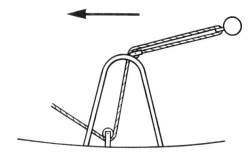

Fig 13   A hoop arrangement for the mainsheet pulls the boom sideways rather than down into the cockpit.

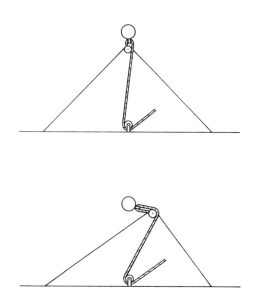

Fig 14   Adjustable strops allow the boom to be positioned on the centre line with very little downwards force. In light air, shorten the windward strop and pull the boom to the centre. This will allow maximum twist as there will be very little downwards force.

adjustable strops is that you shorten the windward strop and allow the boom to sit on the centre line of the boat without any down force.

The only disadvantage of this system is that you have to readjust the strops every time that you tack. As more and more manufacturers' one-designs are appearing, the options that you have on mainsheets are fewer. The RS 400 has a hoop system, while the Laser 5000 and Laser 4000 have fixed strops. Both systems allow the efficient sheeting of the mainsail.

KICKING STRAP

Called by several names, the kicking strap, kicker, vang, or even Gnav (downward pushing) on the Laser 4000, is the primary system for controlling the twist in the mainsail or leech shape. It comes into its own as soon as we move off the wind, as it is the only means of controlling the leech of the sail. While beating, the mainsheet tension will control the leech shape as well as the kicker. In this situation, the one that is tensioned the hardest will have the most impact on the leech. In lighter winds I would recommend that you have no kicker upwind and simply control the boom sideways position and leech shape with the mainsheet. Once on a reach or run, then leech shape will be controlled by you applying the kicker, the mainsheet controlling the boom angle. In stronger winds, when you are playing the mainsheet all the time, you will need to pre-set the kicker. Then, as you ease the mainsheet, the leech profile will stay constant as the boom is eased away from the centre line. Remember that the mainsheet will only affect the leech shape as it starts to pull

downwards in the vicinity of the centre of the boat. Once eased it will only control the boom angle and power. The kicking strap is probably the most important control which is not played constantly. The mainsheet and the jib sheet in a two-person boat, along with the spinnaker sheet downwind, are the only sheets played continuously. Due to its importance, the kicker should be placed in a prominent position, as it is on all the new generation of boats.

CUNNINGHAM

Most people believe that this is a cosmetic control. It is usually attached to the luff of the mainsail 20cm (8in) above the boom. A simple purchase system allows the tensioning of the leading edge of the sail. Often creases will appear in the sail, but unless you are overpowered (hiking as hard as possible and having to play the mainsheet too much), then you should not use the cunningham. If you are overpowered it is a great way of depowering the mainsail. Particularly with the introduction of the fully battened mainsail, this control is increasing in versatility. By pulling on the leading edge of the mainsail we can create extra twist in the head of the sail. This will de-power the sail and make the boat easier to keep upright. It also has an effect on the position of the fullness in the sail, which will be beneficial in over-powered conditions. Next time you are out sailing in full power conditions simply play with the cunningham to understand its effect on the mainsail. It will differ from boat to boat and that is why it is important to understand how it works in specific conditions and in your particular boat.

OUTHAUL

This controls the depth or power in the sail. Its biggest effect is in the bottom part of the sail. Many very detailed books have been written just on rig settings and controls, so I will not try to duplicate them. More and more information is available from the builders of boats, sailmakers or the class associations on how to get the best performance from each different type of boat. For specific information consult these information sources.

FEEDBACK AND STEERING

Just sailing in a straight line is a complex operation, as we have to balance the boat, steer the course we desire and know how to sheet the sails. To aid us in this process we do receive feedback from the boat and our body senses. Our own balance system and feedback from the angle of the boat in relation to the water will allow us to keep the boat upright. Suffice to say that we work as hard as possible to keep the boat level. When this is no longer possible due to the wind strength, we must start to de-power the rig or play the mainsail and jib.

The course we steer will be dictated by the helm, unless we are beating to windward. Here the course will be as high as the wind will allow us to point, with the helm having few options. In order to receive feedback from the sails, they will normally have tell tales fitted. These are small pieces of wool or thin strips of spinnaker nylon. Normally placed 10–15cm

from the luff of the sail, they are approximately 40cm from the foot or in a position where it suits your line of sight. If in doubt, look at some of the other boats in your fleet. Let us imagine that we are sailing on a beat and looking at the tell tales on the jib. We will concentrate on the windward tell tales. If they stall and start to jump around then we are pointing too high. If the leeward tell tales stall then we are pointing too low. (You can normally see the leeward tell tales through the sail.) To be at the optimum point of sailing, the tell tales on both sides should be streaming aft and just flying slightly above the horizontal. Again, you will find that this will vary from boat to boat as the jib cloths and shape will influence how the jib behaves. If the jib is made from a very soft responsive material, then as you steer too high the sail will billow to windward as well as the tell tales stalling.

This method of trimming can also be used on a free leg of the course where the steering is fixed and the sails are trimmed to the wind. The wind is very rarely constant, hence when beating we have to make changes to our steering, and on free legs where steering is fixed make changes to the sails. The crew can trim the sails using the feedback from the tell tales. Ease out the jib too far and the leeward tell tales stall. Pull the jib in too far and the windward tell tales stall, so you will then have to ease out again until both sides are flying just above the horizontal. Fast dinghy sailing is about attention to detail, so you will find that the best crews constantly trim the sails to keep them at their optimum position.

6

Tacking

The simplest manoeuvre that will enable us to turn a dinghy around is the tack. It will be the first method taught to you in the sailing school. The opposite of the tack is the gybe, where we turn away from the wind, rather than passing through head to wind. Although the tack is harder to perform it is none the less a safer manoeuvre. The reason for this is mainly due to commitment, as you will need to have a certain amount of boat speed to pass through head to wind.

The first point to remember about tacking is that you need speed, particularly as the weather conditions become windier, regardless of whether you are on a transom or a centre main dinghy. In order to maintain the speed into the tack, you will have to keep sitting out until the last moment. When that precise moment is will become clear as I talk you through the tacking sequence for both transom and centre main boats, though we will concentrate on centre main boats as this is now the most popular system.

To tack successfully it is important that you have the dinghy under control and upright (*see* Chapter 5). In order to improve your tacking you need to practise away from other boats and in a part of the lake or sea where you are not close to the shore. This will allow you to make a mistake and have another go before you are faced with the task of having to tack for the bank or shore. The less pressure we place on our technique, the quicker we will master these skills and maintain high levels of confidence. As you are sailing along in a straight line, close hauled, practise taking power out of the boat by luffing very slightly. Allow the tell tales on the jib to stream upwards or, if in a singlehander, allow the luff of the sail to blow slightly to windward. This is a very subtle move, only a matter of 3–5 degrees: feel how you can put on or take off power. This will be the key to your tacking.

CENTRE MAIN TACKING
(Figs 15–22)

For the purpose of this chapter we will consider tacking in a doublehander, concentrating on the helm. The first tack to consider will be in a centre main boat, such as a Laser 4000 or singlehanded Laser:

1. Maintain a close-hauled course with the boat upright and as much speed as possible.
2. Make sure that the mainsheet is clear and not wrapped around your feet. Un-cleat the mainsail.
3. Check around you, making sure that you will be clear of other boats once you have tacked.

4. Put the tiller over to about 45 degrees, pushing the tiller extension forward and through the gap between yourself and the mainsheet coming down from the boom. Note that on some boats, including the Laser 4000, the tiller extension may have to go behind the helm due to its length.

5. At the same time, start to move across the boat, following the tiller extension. Your front mainsheet hand goes to a position by the mainsheet cleat, thus releasing about 1m of mainsheet.

6. Your tiller extension hand, once past the mainsheet, will start to move upwards and slightly aft, creating room for your body to arrive on the new side-deck. Keep your main hand close to the cleat as you do not need power at this stage.

7. Sit down on the new side-deck and immediately straighten up the tiller to the central position. As you have tacked while looking forward all the time you will now be steering with your hand behind your back. This should not be a problem.

8. You may need to hike or ease a small amount of mainsheet at this stage to try to keep the boat flat as the power comes back onto the rig on the new tack. If you do not keep control at this stage the boat will turn back into the wind, with the possibility that you may tack again.

9. Take your hand with the mainsheet in (now your aft hand) and clamp the mainsheet to the tiller extension.

10. Release the tiller extension from your hand behind your back, bringing it to your front and taking over the mainsheet.

11. Your hand on the tiller and mainsheet should let go of the mainsheet and resume its job of steering with the tiller extension.

12. Settle down, fine tuning the mainsheet position and your steering.

Problems and Practice

The problems that we will encounter in tacking are: getting into 'irons' (stuck head to wind); over-steering and exiting the tack on a close reach; and lack of confidence in steering behind our backs, with the consequence that we rush this section of the tack.

GETTING INTO 'IRONS'

This happens when the dinghy gets stuck head to wind and starts to sail slowly backwards, driven by the wind. The problem occurs if we tack with too little speed, the boat not having enough energy to pass head to wind. If you practise your tacks close to an obstruction, then this is the normal outcome. Due to the obstruction you work with little confidence and no power, and will probably fail to tack. As you sail closer to the obstruction you will be more inclined just to put the tiller down with less and less speed. The usual outcome is that you sail onto the obstruction or end up getting into 'irons'.

First, practise tacking well away from obstructions until totally confident with your tacking ability. Second, if you do get into 'irons' you need to remain calm and follow the following sequence:

1. You are about to go off on the tack which allows you to stay on the same side of the boat that you are presently on.

33

Fig 15   The helm instigates the tack by turning the boat into the wind, starting to depower the boat and allowing the crew to move.

Fig 16   In shallow cockpit boats both helm and crew should stand, rather than sit.

34

Fig 17 The boat is almost head to wind. The power has been taken from the rig, and helm and crew are starting to cross the boat.

Fig 18 Crouch to get under the boom, but do not sit as the emphasis is on mobility.

Fig 19   The rudder is starting to straighten as the boat exits the tack. Notice
how the helm is now steering behind his back.

Fig 20   As the crew finds the trapeze handle the helm balances the boat with
the mainsheet tension and continues to steer behind his back.

Fig 21   Rudder is straight and the helm moves his mainsheet hand out to the tiller extension at his side.

Fig 22   Clamping the tiller extension with his mainsheet hand, he can now move his forward hand back around to his front and take over the mainsheet, finally letting go of the mainsheet with his back hand.

2. Push the boom away from you by simply reaching upwards. This will give you greater speed backwards.
3. Push the tiller away from you. This action combined with the increase in speed will allow you to reverse out of the tack.
4. Hold this position until the mainsail starts flapping, then start to sheet in the mainsail, as well as pulling the tiller towards you and sitting out.
5. You should now return to your course, increase speed and try the tack again.

If you simply sheet in again without the tiller to windward and do not sit out then the dinghy will simply turn back into the wind. This is due to the turning effect that the sails have. Sheet in the mainsail and the dinghy will turn into the wind. Sheet the jib hard while easing the mainsail and the dinghy will turn away from the wind. In this way the dinghy can be sailed with no rudder, turning the boat with sail forces. Our body weight can also add to the steering effect. If the boat is heeled to windward, then the boat bears away, while conversely if the boat is heeled to leeward, it turns into the wind. We will use these features in more advanced manoeuvres. Suffice to say that you do need to sit out to keep the boat upright, which will counteract the turning into the wind caused by pulling in the mainsheet as we exit sailing in 'irons'. The key to tacking and sailing backwards is to practise. Try sailing backwards when you have mastered the basics of tacking and gybing. Try this in winds of less than force 2 and you will be amazed how much fun it is and how it improves your understanding of how the dinghy sails.

OVER-STEERING

Once you exit the tack, check how close you come out to your new close-hauled course. At first you may find that you exit the tack on more of a close reach than close-hauled. This is due to the tiller being over for too long. Look at where you hold the tiller extension. If the tiller extension is long, as is common on Lasers, you may be forcing the rudder over too far. It's all a case of using levers, so experiment by holding the tiller extension in different positions. As your tiller extension hand passes the mainsheet coming down from the boom, then force it more forwards towards the bow of the boat. This will again have the effect of turning the boat less and reducing the over-steering. If this problem persists, ask the local coach or instructor to take a look at your tacking. Finally remember that the dinghy only needs to turn through 90 degrees or less from tack to tack. The rudder acts as a break, so the less rudder movement we use the less speed we will take from the boat.

STEERING BEHIND YOUR BACK

Steering behind your back is the part of tacking or gybing with a centre main that most people dread. In actual fact all we have to do to overcome this is to prove that this is no different from steering in front of your body. Again, like all of my practice routines, make sure you have plenty of space and the right conditions (less than force 3). After tacking, simply sail on steering the boat with your hand behind your back. Sail for as long as you need to become comfortable; you can still play the mainsheet with your other hand to respond to gusts. Build up confidence in any area of your tacking that you feel needs attention. In this way, when you do arrive at a difficult boat-handling situation you know that you will have the skills to get you through the tack.

TRANSOM MAIN TACKING

As stated earlier, the main difference with transom main is that you do not have to steer behind your back, but you do look aft in all tacks and gybes. The sequence is as follows:

1. Make sure you have total control of the boat by attention to steering, sitting out and mainsheet tension (see point no. 1 in tacking with the centre main system).
2. By clamping the main sheet with your thumb on the tiller extension, swap your front hand onto the tiller extension.
3. Lift the mainsheet away from the tiller extension with your aft hand in preparation for tacking.

Key Points

The positioning of your body and the length of the tiller extension can conflict with each other. This will happen as you try to stop the turning and straighten up the tiller with the extension. Give yourself space to allow this to happen. The mainsheet will also need to be eased as you tack. This is best achieved by allowing your mainsheet hand to move towards the rear of the boat. As you regain your beating position on the new tack pull this mainsheet hand across the body and the mainsheet will be automatically returned to its beating position.

---

4. Push the tiller extension away to instigate the tack, with the tiller going to approximately 45 degrees.
5. Follow the tiller extension with your body, pivoting on your feet to face aft as you cross the dinghy.
6. As you sit down on the new side-deck, ensure that you are as far forward as possible as this creates the space for you to straighten up the tiller extension.
7. If you heel excessively in the tack then the mainsheet can be eased to prevent this.

Special Tacking Techniques

These techniques are based on the fact that the boat can be steered by body weight and sheeting sails. We need to use special techniques in light and strong winds. In these conditions the turning forces generated by the dinghy are either too great or too small to facilitate the most efficient tacking.

Strong Winds

The key to tacking in strong winds is commitment and keeping the boat very flat. As soon as the boat heels it will slow up and have less force to overcome the waves, which will have been created by the wind. If the boat should stall in the tack, you can try to help the bow around by backing the jib. In this instance you will have passed head to wind, but then run out of speed to take the boat around to the new tack. Prior to the boat going into 'irons' you can sheet the jib on its original tack. The jib will invert as the wind is in effect coming from the wrong side. The bow of the boat will blow around very rapidly and the jib will need to be released extremely quickly to stop the boat being blown over in a capsize.

Light Winds

The roll tack was developed to allow more efficient tacking in light winds. It uses the limited forces generated in light winds to turn the boat without using the rudder and slowing the boat. Upon entering the tack the boat is heeled away from the wind, which turns the boat into the wind. Depending upon your type of dinghy, you may need to use some limited amounts of rudder to instigate the turn. As the boat reaches head to wind body weight is applied to the windward side of the dinghy. This propels the boat past head to wind and onto the new tack. Rudder movements will be needed to facilitate this.

All of this movement requires a great deal of coordinated crew movements. The crew may need to go to leeward to instigate the first heel to leeward. Then move to the windward side, cross the boat as it tacks, pulling the boat upright with body weight. Finally, move to the leeward side to stop the boat from heeling too much to windward. The rules recognize that this may aid forward movement as it is such an efficient means of tacking. However you cannot exit the tack faster than you entered, stopping it as a means of forward propulsion. The keys to roll tacking are:

1. Allow the boat to turn to head to wind before you apply the weight to the windward side. This does take some time, though applying weight too early will not give you the propulsion through the tack and it will feel flat.
2. Movements must be as coordinated and as smooth as possible. Clumsy movements about the boat will reduce your speed.
3. Immediately after the tack, ease the sheets on the sails, allowing the boat to return to maximum speed before pointing onto your close-hauled course. Momentum is the name of the game in drifting conditions, so never point high until you have the speed.

7
Gybing

For some reason, which is probably the speed with which the boom crosses the boat, gybing is feared more than tacking by dinghy sailors. This is not always the case with beginners – just watch a group of youngsters out sailing in Optimists and they invariably gybe because they find it easier than tacking. Within this chapter I will describe how we can gybe in centre and transom main dinghies and come up with some simple practice sessions which hopefully will allow you to gybe as confidently and freely as you do tack.

CENTRE MAIN GYBING
(Figs 23–30)

As you will have read, I prefer the centre main to the transom. This is simply because I like to see where I am positioning the boat during all manoeuvres. It is purely a personal matter, and unless the rules constrain you, then the mainsheet system should reflect your individual preference. Preparation is again the key to gybing, as I feel that if you are in control of the situation, the sequence will flow as you wish. It is only when we put stress on our

Fig 23   Have control as you enter the gybe.

Fig 24 The tiller extension goes across first, followed by the helm. Note how upright the boat is.

Fig 25 Gybe at maximum speed as this will result in the least load on the mainsail, allowing it to cross the boat easily. Help it on its way with the mainsheet.

Fig 26   As the boom comes across, start to straighten the tiller to stop the boat turning. We want to exit on a broad reach or run.

Fig 27   The boom has crossed the boat and the tiller is being corrected to put the boat on as broad a reach as is possible.

43

Fig 28   The helm is steering behind his back and is moving out onto the wings to flatten the boat.

Fig 29   No heel is now on the boat and the helm is swapping his mainsheet and tiller hands. You do not need to rush this manoeuvre: practise sailing with your tiller extension behind your back.

Fig 30   Both hands are working on the mainsheet to trim the mainsail. The tiller extension hand acts as a cleat.

boat-handling ability that the mistakes occur. It does not matter what ability level you have reached, the more in control you are, the easier the manoeuvre.

Approaching the spot where you wish to gybe you must be in control; if not, you must regain control. If the boat is rolling, sheet in on the mainsheet and luff up slightly. It may be that too much twist is in the mainsail and this is causing the rolling. Correct this by pulling on the kicking strap. As you enter the gybe you should be on a broad reach. If you are sailing any tighter than this you will need to turn through a very large angle. From the broad reach, follow this sequence:

1. Check that there is no boat on your inside: you will need a clear space to gybe into. Sheet in the mainsheet to over-sheet the mainsail (depends on boat/see hints).
2. The gybe will be controlled by rudder movements. These should be positive. Pass the tiller extension through the gap between the mainsheet and your body. Your body should be crouching and following the tiller extension. Alternatively, with long tiller extensions, put it around behind you.
3. This action will start the boat turning, while your weight following the extension will maintain the boat in a very upright position. The boat angle is important to stop the forces generated from heeling taking over. We talked about these in Chapter 6.
4. The boat needs to turn at least 30 degrees before the wind will start to affect the leech of the mainsail. This is the reason that we over-sheet the sail to allow this to happen earlier.
5. If you are sailing in a dinghy with all the parts of the mainsheet in front of you, these can be pulled across the boat to aid the boom crossing the dinghy. In

45

boats like a Laser where the 2:1 main-sheet purchase is on the transom, this action has very little effect so steering must be very precise. In a two-person dinghy, the crew can aid the boom across by pulling on the kicking strap. (This is no longer possible in boats such as the Laser 4000, as the Gnav is used to create more space for the crew.)

6. The key to successful gybing is to be aware of when the boom is starting to move across the boat. As soon as this happens you need to straighten up the tiller to stop the boat continuing to turn. The aim is to have the boat on a broad reach or run by the time the boom exerts tension on the mainsheet on the new gybe.

7. During this steering you will still have the tiller extension behind your back, just as in tacking. This should not be a problem, particularly if you practise steering in this way.

8. Take your mainsheet hand to the tiller extension, clamp the mainsheet and release your old tiller extension hand, moving it around your body and regaining control of the mainsheet.

9. Body position is crucial to keeping the boat upright, so beware of too much weight to windward after the gybe. The more accurate you are with the steering, the less weight you will need. If the boat is still turning after the boom has come across, then you will need lots of weight as the boat will continue to turn and heel.

Getting It Right *(Fig 31)*

Gybing is all about the transfer of forces from one side to the other. Due to the speed with which the forces transfer, it can be difficult to evaluate this sequence.

However, if we understand these forces then we can cope with them. The first force to understand is that the slower your boat is travelling, then the larger the load on the rig. Therefore we need commitment and we need speed. If you are sailing on a large piece of water the waves will offer the solution. As you are picked up by a wave, perhaps even surfing, your speed increases. As speed increases the load on the rig decreases. If you ever see a catamaran travelling quickly, and then gybing, it is as if the crew have just placed the boom on the other side as they gybe. They were probably gybing at a speed equivalent to the wind speed. If you drive downwind on a motor boat at ten knots and the wind is 10 knots from behind, then it will feel as if there is *no* wind! This is what we want to achieve: as little wind load on the rig as possible. The key is to gybe when in control and at your fastest, on a wave if possible.

Maintaining the boat upright is the second key. As we have seen in Chapter 6, as the boat heels it aids the steering, whereas if the boat is very level then the forces are virtually neutral. The boat heeling coming out of the gybe is what we do not want, as it will continue to turn, generating more heeling. Due to the angle of heel it will be very hard to release the pressure in the mainsail by easing the mainsheet. The boom will run out spilling wind until it hits the water, whereupon it cannot release any more pressure. The end result is even more heeling and turning, and a capsize may be the eventual result.

Steering is the final and most precise area. As I have stated, we want the wind to act on the new side of the mainsail, thus forcing the boom across the boat. This is the strongest force we have to move the

Fig 31 If we get the balance wrong, the boom is pinned by the water creating too much power and turning and the boat will capsize.

boom. If you see crews struggling in a gybe, it is usually because they are fighting this force. It may be a crew pulling desperately on the kicking strap or helm pulling on the mainsheet without using enough rudder. Either way they are fighting the force. The kicking strap is not a very efficient lever with which to pull the boom across; half-way down the boom by the mainsheet will give you much better leverage. Timing is the important factor as we will instigate the boom moving by turning the boat. As soon as the boom is 'on its way' across the boat, we need to resume

47

the course on a broad reach or preferably a run. You will feel this change of force in the pressure on the mainsheet. The specific forces will vary from each boat, although if you understand the forces and let your senses be aware of changes you will soon develop a feeling for gybing. With this feeling will come confidence, the result being that you will no longer know how you gybe, it will just happen naturally as the whole process become intuitive rather than a planned sequence of actions.

TRANSOM MAIN/GYBING

The forces are the same, but the sequence is slightly different:

1. Approach the point where you wish to gybe in control with the boat upright.
2. Approach on a broad reach and over-sheet the mainsheet.
3. Swap the tiller extension and main-sheet hand as with tacking.
4. Separate the hands, moving the tiller extension across the boat while squatting and pivoting, facing aft.
5. As the tiller extension is forced across the boat this will turn the tiller to about 45 degrees.
6. As the boat starts to turn, you should concentrate on balancing the boat by keeping it upright. This will mean that you are now squatting in the middle of the boat.
7. Eventually the wind will apply a force to the new side of the mainsail and start to move the boom across the boat.
8. As soon as this happens, cancel the turning by straightening up the tiller with the tiller extension. A good clue as to when this is happening is to feel

the pressure on the mainsheet or to look at the mainsheet. As soon as the load starts to come off move the tiller extension.

9. As the tiller extension is used to straighten the boat, continue to pivot on your toes, turning forwards and sitting down.
10. The amount of weight on the wind-ward side is again related to the accuracy of your turning. If it was perfect you will need very little weight but if the turning was stopped too late you will need to counteract the turning with your body weight.

ROLL GYBING

In light winds, gybing can be aided by the rolling of the boat. The movement of the crew's body weight is used to aid the turning of the boat and also aid the moving of the boom from one gybe to the other. In order to carry out this manoeuvre, follow the following sequence:

1. In light air you may be sailing with the boat heeled away from the wind to reduce the wetted area, as well as giving you some feel on the rudder.
2. As you bear away to gybe, heel the boat to windward. This has two consequences: the boat will bear away and the speed of the boat will be accelerated by your movement.
3. Despite the light winds, you will probably find that the boom is now propelled across the dinghy.
4. As the boom comes across, you will need to swap sides very quickly as well as nimbly in order to keep the momentum going.
5. The boom will have reached its limit as

dictated by the mainsheet length. As it gets to this point the boat is brought upright and the main is sheeted in and trimmed to the correct position.

6. The dinghy should now be on its new course with the same speed that you entered the gybe. Remember the rules stop us from using this manoeuvre repeatedly and you can only exit the gybe at the same speed with which you entered.

'The physical techniques you need to have learned to be successful at gybing in strong winds are not difficult. What is essential is that you decide who is in charge, you or the boat – are you riding or driving?'

Shirley Robertson, GBR Europe sailor, 1992 Olympics

Fig 32   Shirley Robertson, GBR Europe representative at the 1992 Olympic games, Barcelona, Spain.

8

The Trapeze

As we progress in the sport of dinghy sailing we move into higher-performance boats. Frequently these boats will have a trapeze. More junior boats are designed with trapezing in mind and so the subsequent generation of adult boats also features the trapeze as standard. All sport and leisure activities in the 1990s are being geared to generate more excitement and take shorter periods of our valuable leisure time. The trapeze is one such device: it is easy to use and considerably improves the performance of modern-day dinghies. Combine this with a system of wings to increase the righting moment of the boat with crew weight equalization, and excitement increases quite dramatically! The important point about the trapeze is that it should not intimidate the user, so we have to devise a safe way for people to become familiar with the systems.

THE EQUIPMENT *(Fig 33)*

Trapeze gear has become standardized during the 1990s, and now consists of an adjustable-height purchase system attached below the trapeze handle. The choice of handle is still a debatable point, with the open 'L' handle becoming increasingly popular. This is more expensive than other handles but has some significant advantages. Another option is the

plastic bar, threaded through the trapeze wire. Cheap and lightweight it may be, but it is hard to grab as you have to decide how many fingers go each side of the wire. It never looks very substantial, despite the fact that it is strong enough. The other handle is the enclosed stainless steel or alloy handle. This definitely looks substantial enough, but you do need to be very accurate with your hand placement when grabbing the handle.

The 'L' handle allows ease of grabbing from any angle, with crews using the vertical or horizontal bar. Below this handle is the adjustable-height hook. Normally controlled by a 2:1 adjustable system, a specifically designed cleat made by Clamcleat is proving very popular. The cleat has no working parts and is very positive in cleating, giving a definite cleated or not-cleated position. The rope adjustment should have a stopper knot to stop the rope from running through if released. This should be 100mm from the end of the rope to allow ease of gripping when the system is fully extended.

The systems will become specific to the crews using them. Handle height is important to facilitate ease of movement with minimum effort. To check the handle height, you should be able to grab the handle with a straight arm by bending your upper body slightly from the horizontal. The adjustment should be at its longest. The reason for this is that as you

Fig 33 Adjusting the nappy style of harness, incorporating a spreader bar.

end of the adjustable system, so some rope will be left. This is used as you go onto a reach. As you move back in the boat your height changes and you will find yourself in a more upright position. To return to a lower, more powerful position you ease the final part of the height adjuster. At its final position, with the stopper knot in the cleat, you should be in a low position and have moved aft in the boat.

This is for the future; to start with, you will want to progress slowly, building confidence as you go. The harness is the final piece of the equipment that you must have confidence in. The most popular harnesses are adjustable, not only around the body but also to accommodate differing heights. A spreader bar developed in windsurfing is becoming more popular as the system for connecting you and your harness to the adjustable-height hook. Both systems provide a positive way in connecting the two. If your harness has a small 'rubber' retaining device below the hook, then I would suggest that this be removed to allow easier tacking. The system that you can use when combined with the height adjuster makes the retainer obsolete and it will actually hinder your tacking. The key to the harness is comfort, so try it on wearing the wet suit or dry suit that you normally wear while sailing. The side adjusters should be adjusted to be snug around your hips.

A trend has started for individual harnesses to be worn by the top crews. These 'nappy' harnesses, as they are called, are put on by wriggling into them as they have limited length or no side adjusters. This wriggling will give you some idea of how to adjust the tension of your side adjusters. If you can wriggle in,

progress in trapeze technique you can hook on while out on the wire. The easiest way to perfect this is to hang with a straight arm.

The adjustable-height system will be very useful in light conditions where you want to work while in a very high, upright position. The other extreme is where you want to exert maximum righting movement in stronger winds. This will place you at right angles to the mast in a horizontal position. Hopefully the helm will be playing the mainsheet to keep the boat upright and the crew will be parallel to the water, just above the waves. In the beating position you will not be at the

51

it's about right. The straps that go over your shoulders should be easy to adjust. To check the tension in these, you should feel your weight being taken on them as you fully extend your body in the trapeze position. Too loose and your back will arch, which is very bad. Too tight and you will be hunched up in a ball and feel very uncomfortable. You may wish to readjust this shoulder strap after getting out on the trapeze for the first time as the system does tend to 'bed-in' and allow for a small amount of movement. After finishing the race, before getting to the launching ramp you will probably want to ease a similar amount of tension.

CONFIDENCE *(Fig 34)*

Confidence is the key to trapezing, and recognizing your own attitude will be a factor in maintaining confidence as you learn to trapeze. It is great fun and opens up a new and exciting element to modern dinghy sailing. If you are a carefree type of person who thinks bungee jumping is good fun, then you haven't a worry and you may as well start on the water. If you are a more cautious type, I would suggest some dry land simulation prior to starting on the water. No one way is right. The right way is the one that suits you. Another alternative is learning from a stable base such as a catamaran, which is frequently used by well-equipped sailing schools for this purpose.

The trapeze is an aid to your movement around the boat and should not be viewed as something that you clip onto as the boat starts to heel. Even in light winds, where the crew may be moving from inside the boat to fully hiking, I would use the trapeze to aid this move-

ment. Simply hook on while sitting on the side of the boat, adjust the height adjusters so that you skim the deck and just experience your weight being taken by the trapeze. You do not need to hang on to the handle, just relax and let the harness do the work. Once you have mastered this swinging feeling, you should be able to position yourself to balance the boat simply by pushing off anything in the boat.

I think that we are too constrained by learning from a set technique. In lighter winds you may trapeze off the top of the centreboard case if this is in a suitable position. Why hunch yourself up on the side of the gunwale with your legs bent and in an uncomfortable position? Alternatively, you could have straight legs, trapezing off the case top and be in the same position. This form of 'open' thinking towards trapezing will enable you to make transitional moves much easier. So often you see crews struggling to move out from the gunwale to the trapeze position. They are invariably making three mistakes:

1. They are not allowing the trapeze gear to take the load, as they are desperately taking their weight on the handle (frequently with two hands).
2. They are on too low a hook position.
3. They are struggling from an awkward position on the gunwale due to using the gunwale to push off from.

The solution is to *relax*: enjoy this new skill. Go high on the adjusters to start with. Do not sit down, but use the trapeze as a swing to move around the boat, and push off from the mast, the case top, the helm, or anything that will aid your ability to balance the boat.

Fig 34   The crew in a very mobile high-hook position allowing him to walk around the deck to balance the boat. Note the L-shaped trapeze handle.

A STANDARD SYSTEM
(Figs 35–40)

Describing a standard method will allow you to have some structure in your practice. The key to this is that the trapeze should feel like a swing, you should take all your weight with you and you should decide in what position you want to be. The high position, with your bottom just skimming the deck, is the position to start in. Hook on while sitting on the side-deck and adjust your height to this position. You will find that due to the forces involved in trapezing you will be pulled forward in the boat. To counter this you will always need more tension in your leading leg than in your rear leg. This will vary from boat to boat and can simply be compensated for by slightly bending your rear leg. You will also find that the forces on the water caused by the boat moving forward will be different from those experienced on dry land. Ideally you should first trapeze on a close reach. In this aspect of sailing, an experienced helm will be able to compensate for your weight going on the trapeze by playing the mainsheet. As you go out on the trapeze and need more power in the rig to balance you, the helm can apply power by sheeting the mainsheet.

From your floating position on the side-deck, push out over the side of the boat. This should be as smooth a movement as possible, concentrating on maintaining pressure on the front leg. Any part of the boat can be used for this procedure; indeed you may find enough grip on the deck itself. Try to use something to initiate this push that will place you slightly outside the boat. Then from this position it will be easy for your front leg to find the gunwale and propel you out to the fully extended position. A problem can occur if the initial push does not get you far enough outboard for the foot to find the gunwale. You may find yourself too hunched up and then your leg will struggle to generate the power to propel you out to the full position. With the new generation of racked boats there appear to be many options for pushing out. The final choice will depend upon rack size and your flexibility and comfort.

Once out in the fully extended position, simply relax and enjoy the start of high-performance dinghy sailing! As you begin to develop confidence and balance, your feet will move closer together and the difference in pressure between your two feet will decrease. Practise moving in and out on the wire as this is how you will balance the boat as it responds to gusts. If you do ever feel yourself going forward, bend your rear leg and straighten your front leg, or alternatively just grab the helm. When it comes to tacking and coming in from the trapeze, get the helm to ease off the power with the mainsail and swing in. Your speed will again be controlled by your legs. The front leg will bend, while the rear leg moves over the gunwale and into the boat. As you are on a high hook you will need to take your weight on the handle to brush the hook off. As you progress to a lower hook the unhooking will become easier.

The new generation of dinghies with self-draining floors and cockpits makes trapezing easier as it is easier to push out. The boats have no real lip created by the side of the boat as they are more dish-like. This is both an advantage and a disadvantage. The advantage is the ease of trapezing, while the disadvantage is only for those who like sitting down. If you sit down it will be hard to move. The crucial point is that you should use the trapeze

Fig 35   Hook on while on the side deck and then push out with the front leg.

Fig 36 Keep more pressure on your front leg as the forces will want to ease you towards the bow.

Fig 37 Once fully out, settle back and let the harness take the load.

Fig 38 When coming back into the boat, simply control your speed with your legs.

Fig 39 As you ease into the boat, take some of the load on the handle.

Fig 40 Finally knock the hook off the harness in preparation for a tack. Cut off the rubber retainer from the harness as this stops the hook coming off the harness easily.

as a method of moving, not something that you hook into when you need it.

MORE ADVANCED TECHNIQUES *(Figs 41–50)*

Trapeze technique will progress very quickly as long as you find the right environment to keep building your confidence. Once the basics have been mastered then progressing on to smoother tacks can be achieved. Again, work on the system for your particular boat and the way it has been laid out. Some crews will tack facing backwards, while some will face forwards. This will depend on where the turning block is for the jib. Tack facing aft if the turning

block is aft and forwards if it is forwards. Once tacking has been accomplished, then the final stage is to perfect tacking and hooking on once out on the trapeze. Although at first this sounds and looks as if it should only be performed within a circus big top, it is very easy to achieve for both male and female crews. Again it revolves around a few simple rules:

1. Make sure the trapeze handle is comfortable and at the right height to allow your weight to be taken on a straight arm.
2. Make sure the leading front hand always goes to the handle, while the rear hand attends to the jib.
3. Push out as quickly as possible on completion of the tack, thus allowing the mainsail power to be kept on in the tack.
4. Once out, cleat the jib, then without dropping the jib sheet move this hand to the hook, while still hanging on the front hand (this arm must be straight).
5. Hook on and release the front hand from the handle.

For high-speed tacking, the reverse is carried out:

1. Front hand goes to the handle as you start to move in.
2. Rear hand un-cleats the jib as you are swinging into the boat.
3. Rear hand sweeps the hook out of the harness, which is much easier if the rubber retainer has been removed. (The trapeze elastic may have already removed the hook as you take the load on your arm).
4. Jib is just starting to flap as you move across the boat. Pick up the new jib sheet and go into the sequence above.

57

Fig 41 Going out on the handle is a quicker method of tacking. Simply take your weight on the handle and push out.

Fig 42 As soon as you are out, take the load on a straight arm rather than a bent arm.

Fig 43 Find the hook and clip it onto your harness.

Fig 44 Once hooked on you can settle down and release the handle.

Fig 45 Tacking the shallow cockpit designs requires you to stand as you tack. Communication is vital between helm and crew.

Fig 46   As you start the tack take the load on the handle and the trapeze
elastic will take the hook away from your harness.

Fig 47   Start to walk into the boat,
aiding your balance with the jib sheet
and trapeze handle.

Fig 48   The jib will be uncleated as
the boat turns into the wind, so pre-
pare to duck down under the boom.

Fig 49   Only drop to one knee, trying to keep on your feet, as mobility is the key to tacking in shallow cockpit boats.

SPEED AND PRACTICE
(Figs 51–3)

All of these manoeuvres if performed at high speed will allow modern dinghies to be driven very hard and achieve their expected level of performance. If these are performed slowly they will not work. If you try to tack slowly without releasing the jib then the boat will heel a lot and broach, with the rudder stalling. They are specific actions to be used in a specific sequence and at a specific speed. You cannot compromise them, so progress at a speed which your skill-level and confidence dictate. This may mean close communication between helm and crew and you will find that carefully constructed goals will resolve any problems in this area. If you enjoy the sailing you will progress very quickly, particularly with the right advice. If

Fig 50   Find the handle and get out as quickly as possible so that the helm can sheet the mainsail and develop the power. The crew can now hook on.

Fig 51   Wire to wire tacking from in front, shows the crew straight arm hanging from the handle.

you are scared of the boat because your confidence has drained, then progress will be slow and painful. Forget any thoughts of putting your hands above your head until you are 100 per cent happy in your

manoeuvre and tacking handle to handle! Take one step at a time, as having the hands on the head is a marginal advantage for those who are totally experienced in the art of trapezing.

Fig 52   The crew bends his legs slightly as he hooks on.

Fig 53   Hooked into the harness the crew can adjust the height adjuster to drop his body position down to parallel with the water.

9

Spinnakers – Asymmetric and Conventional

As you will already have discovered, I am a great advocate of the asymmetric spinnaker. As far as I am concerned, it has brought about easier handling, faster speeds and much more fun to the downwind legs of sailing. At the same time as the asymmetric was being introduced to dinghy sailing through the new manufacturers' one-designs, the whole concept of sailing was being reviewed. To a certain extent this was driven by the IYRU (International Yacht Racing Union) as it fought to make sailing a more exciting Olympic sport. In the past, conventional Olympic sailing took place away from the shore line to ensure the fairest winds. The course was a large triangular one with legs in excess of one mile. The duration of the race could be anything from slightly under two hours to five hours, depending upon how strong the wind was. The complaint from the sailors, as well as the media, was that the races were often decided on the first leg and after that all that took place was a long procession with little opportunity to overtake.

The reasons for this were many. The length of the first leg allowed massive separation of the fleet, resulting in large gains and losses. The speed differences on the reaches presented the only opportunity to overtake, as tactics had very little to do with overtaking. Finally it took a long time to sail to and from the course and no spectators could ever see the race, even if they could understand it. Dinghy racing was particularly hard to watch as the course (consisting of only three marks) was not clearly marked.

During the years 1993 and 1994 many different courses, as well as formats of racing, were experimented with. These included races for ten-boat fleets, having been whittled down on a knock-out basis, to fleets of 120 all sailing together. The knock out was not enjoyed by the sailors because most of a week's sailing competition would count for nothing, the final result being decided on a few races in very specific wind conditions on one or two days. Sailing is an open sport where a long series with at least one discardable race gives the fairest results. The sailors may not have liked the knock out, but they loved the shorter races with a finish at the bottom of the course. This is the opposite of the conventional pre-1992 Olympic courses, where races were finished on a beat. Now it was downwind, which had two advantages: first, you finish at the bottom of the course, so no time at all is needed to start another race; and second, spectators could see who was winning, as all boats were sailing the same straight course rather than tacking upwind at strange angles.

The races were also shorter as the course length was now set to give 40–45 minute races. In stronger winds a larger course was set. A normal day's race was much closer to the shore, with up to three races sailed one after another – about three hours' racing, which was adequate for all competitors. In a four-day series there could be twelve races with at least one discard. The maximum number of boats that these smaller courses could accommodate was about fifty to sixty. If there were more than this, you sailed in fleets with the top sixty sailing in the Gold fleet and the next sixty in the Silver fleet. It is imperative that all sailors get an equal amount of racing, whether they are in the Gold or Silver fleet.

These formats are still being refined in early 1995, but the one major difference in course design has been the introduction of more running than reaching. This has brought back tactical sailing to the downwind leg and allows much place-changing. It is now a great test of tactical positioning and speed.

As these courses were being developed so too was the asymmetric spinnaker, which was originally developed by Julian Bethwaite for his Eighteen Foot Skiff in Australia. Other classes continued the development, most significantly the International 14 in the UK, but it was the introduction of the ISO from Topper International and then the Laser 5000, RS 400 and Laser 4000 which marked its arrival for the masses. The asymmetric is not designed to run but to reach, so it appears a little ironic that as the runs are increased in sailing, this design starts to predominate. In actual fact the skill with an asymmetric is to balance the trade-off between going higher and sailing faster and further, or going lower and sailing slower and less far. It is this interesting dichotomy and the introduction of apparent wind into the equation that makes it so stimulating, as well as being a lot of fun. Also introduced by designer Phil Morrison with the RS 400 and Laser 4000 was the concept of adjusting the bowsprit (asymmetric spinnaker pole) angle to windward away from the centre line to allow deeper running.

An integral part of the asymmetric is the ease of handling, and this is brought about by the removal of the conventional spinnaker pole and the introduction of the bowsprit. This pole is longer than conventional poles, therefore allowing the spinnaker to be set further away from the mainsail than with the conventional set-up. This improves the efficiency of the rig downwind. This bowsprit is stored inside the boat and pulled out of the boat by a rope purchase. On certain boats this action also allows the tack of the spinnaker to be pulled to the outboard end of the pole. The asymmetric spinnaker can best be described as a very full jib, which is controlled by two sheets, one for each side. Control is just as it is for the jib. The bowsprit needs to be held in its extended position by a control line and will be brought back into the boat by the simple act of the crew recovering the spinnaker.

APPARENT WIND *(Fig 54)*

In sailing downwind the apparent wind is becoming increasingly important. The introduction of the asymmetric spinnaker and lighter boats have had this effect. Apparent wind is the wind that we feel as soon as we move. Imagine a train in a station on a windless day. If you hold your hand out of the window you feel no wind. As the train pulls away from the station the wind on your hand increases, this being the apparent wind. The same is true on a dinghy, the important wind being not the true wind but the apparent. This apparent wind is stronger and further forward than true wind, allowing us to sail deeper as we increase the speed of the boat. (More detail on the scientific approach to high-speed sailing can be found in Frank Bethwaite's book *High Performance Sailing*.)

TRIMMING *(Fig 55)*

The advantage of the asymmetric spinnaker is the fact that trimming is the same skill as you will have developed to trim the jib. Both rely upon the constant easing or hardening of the sheet based upon feedback from the sail. In the case of the asymmetric we need to concentrate on the luff (leading edge) of the sail. As you ease the sheet you will note that at a critical point the sail will start to curl. If you continue to ease the sheet, then the sail will continue to curl, eventually collapsing. Each design of asymmetric will behave in a different way, depending upon how tolerant the sail is. Compared to some conventional high-performance spinnaker designs, I have found the recent asymmetric designs for production boats to be very tolerant.

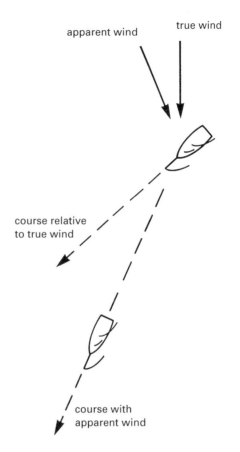

Fig 54   The real sailing wind is the apparent wind, which is stronger and also allows us to sail deeper as it is slightly ahead of the true wind.

The best way to practise trimming the sail is away from the race course. It is important that the crew becomes familiar with the handling of the sail in a low-pressure situation. The aim will be to ease the sheet constantly until the sail just starts to curl (approximately 75mm). As the sail curls to this position the crew simply sheets the sail again to take out the 75mm of curl. Again and again, ease

Fig 55   The skill of trimming spinnakers (asymmetric or normal) is to roll the luff over constantly by sheeting out and then sheet in to flick the luff back.

the sail to create the curled luff. The aim is for the sail to be always operating in the range of just about to curl, which is where it is operating at its most efficient. If we do not trim the sail in this fashion, as long as it is flying and not collapsing, then it may well be over-trimmed. In an over-trimmed position the sail is not operating efficiently and will also generate too large a healing force.

A key point in sheeting these sails is that you will need to over-sheet the sails to get them to fill initially. This will happen on initial hoisting, after the sail collapses, and after gybing. The easing of the sheet just after the sail has filled will become second nature to you as a crew. This will allow you to find the curl/breaking point as soon as possible after any of these manoeuvres. Remember that the sail needs to operate at this critical point all the time in order to develop the maximum performance.

CHUTES AND BAGS

The storage of the spinnaker or asymmetric within the boat offers another opportunity for performance gain. Many a famous dinghy sailor has stated that dinghy sailing is about making the fewest mistakes. When launching or recovering the spinnaker or asymmetric we have a situation where we can make a mistake that will affect our performance. The design of the system that we use can have a bearing on this.

Chutes *(Figs 56–76)*

Spinnaker chutes rely upon drawing the spinnaker or asymmetric into some form of storage device by means of a rope (striker cord or retrieval line). This very lightweight sheet is attached to the spinnaker by means of a reinforced patch. On large sails this may consist of

Fig 56   The helm steers with his knees as he hoists with the crew tending to other sail controls.

Fig 57   As the spinnaker emerges the crew can find the sheet and balance the boat.

Fig 58   The helm pulls the last part of the halyard and the crew can set the spinnaker. The crew should be aware that if the spinnaker is set before the sail is fully hoisted the friction will increase dramatically on the halyard.

Fig 59   The crew starts to move out to balance the boat while the helm takes the tiller.

Fig 60   The helm joins the crew on the racks.

Fig 61   As the apparent wind builds the crew can move out to trapeze off the racks.

Fig 62   An alternative method is for the helm to continue to steer with the crew hoisting the spinnaker.

Fig 63   With the Laser 4000 the one halyard pulls out the bowsprit and hoists the spinnaker.

Fig 64   Spinnaker set: this is a slightly slower but definitely more controlled method of launching the spinnaker.

more than one patch to concertina the sail into a small length.

The hoisting method of all spinnakers/asymmetrics is similar. In a prearranged case the spinnaker pole/ bowsprit is clipped to the mast or pulled out. The guy will already be in the pole end or, in the case of an asymmetric, the tack will have been pulled to the bowsprit end. The spinnaker/asymmetric halyard is now hoisted and the sheet trimmed until the sail fills.

With symmetrical and asymmetric spinnakers, the sheet will need to be eased just after the sail fills in order to provide the most efficient trimming position. When it comes to taking the spinnaker down with the chute system, the sail is pulled down by a line, entering the boat via the chute mouth at the bow of the dinghy. The sail is then stored in some form of specific bag, which may consist of a sausage bag or even a specific area at the front of the boat. The retrieval line can generally be pulled by the helm or crew with the system arranged for either to use. It is normally a continuous system.

73

Fig 65   The more complex conventional spinnaker system. The helm leans forward and pulls on the twinner for the guy. This also pulls the spinnaker partially out of the leeward bag.

Fig 66   The crew swings in from the trapeze to put the spinnaker pole into place. In this boat the rules say that it must be stored in the cockpit.

Fig 67   Crew attaches the uphaul/downhaul system to the pole with a hook.

Fig 68   With a good downhaul system this is the hardest part as you push the pole onto the mast. The guy is in the outer end.

Fig 69   Pole on, the helm can now hoist the spinnaker from the leeward bag. The system used on this boat allows the helm to hoist with just one hand.

Fig 70   Spinnaker set the crew can trapeze, while the helm sorts other controls inside the boat. Note the twinning line cleat by the shroud base which
controls the guy.

Fig 71 On many of the new boats the drop can be performed by either the helm or the crew. Here the helm takes the spinnaker sheet as the crew moves into the boat to drop the spinnaker.

Fig 72 The crew uncleats the halyard and simply pulls on the spinnaker retrieval line.

Fig 73   The spinnaker drops away as the retrieval line can just be seen starting to pull towards the chute mouth at the bow.

Fig 74   Spinnaker and pole are now away in the chute as the crew pulls the
last part of the retrieval line.

Fig 75   Hardening up for the upwind leg, the crew sheets the jib and moves
out on the racks. The helm has had total control through steering and mainsail
trim throughout this manoeuvre.

Fig 76   Fully powered-up, the crew can move out onto the racks. Note the last
section of the bowsprit just visible at the bow

79

Bags *(Figs 77–88)*

The opposite system to this is where the crew retrieves the spinnaker by hand after releasing the spinnaker halyard. The sail is then stored in a central bag or in two bags on either side of the boat. The sail is dropped on the windward side of the dinghy by working down the leech and then stuffing the spinnaker into the bag. In dropping in this fashion, speed is of the essence as this will stop the foot of the sail or the sheet from dropping over the bow. Do not attempt to gather the foot as this will normally result in a twist in the sail on the next hoist. Concentrate on working down the leech, reaching up the leech as far as you can to use as few armfuls as possible to pack the sail. This is also the system used to pack the sail in the dinghy park.

Preparation is the main difference between the two systems. With the bag system you need to think about the next hoist as you drop the sail. The sail should always be dropped in the bag which will allow a hoist from the leeward side on the next hoist, particularly if this will be on a reach. If the next hoist is on a run then either bag can be used, as hoisting from the windward or leeward bag can be performed.

Fig 77   Conventional drop for a boat with spinnaker bags.

Fig 78 Crew moves from the trapeze and takes the spinnaker pole off. With careful steering on the part of the helm the boat can be balanced. (Note that the helm has the spinnaker sheet with the spinnaker still filling.)

Fig 79 The crew grabs the guy and starts to pull the spinnaker towards him.

Fig 80   The helm has let the halyard go while the crew start to work down the leech of the spinnaker.

Fig 81   The crew is still working down the leech as he stuffs the sail into the bag. It is important to work down the leech to avoid twists at the next hoist.

Fig 82   As the crew finishes this job the helm is starting to turn the boat and sheet in the mainsail.

Fig 83   Both main and jib are coming in with the boat being balanced by the crew.

Fig 84   Settled down for the beat, you can see the strops on the mainsheet which allow the boom to be sheeted close to the centreline of the boat.

If the next hoist is a starboard reach, then the spinnaker should be dropped in the port bag. This will dictate how you approach the leeward mark. If you are approaching on a port reach, then you will bring the sail down in the windward port bag, ready for the starboard reach. Should you arrive on a reach where the spinnaker is in the windward bag, the system has to change to accommodate this. The first job is for the spinnaker to be hoisted at the same time as the crew throws the sail in front of the forestay, the wind blowing it around to the leeward side.

Fig 85   With spinnaker bags you may have to hoist from the windward spinnaker bag. Here the spinnaker goes up before we put the pole on the mast.

Fig 86   Good communications are essential. As the crew throws the spinnaker around the forestay in front of the boat the helm hoists.

Fig 87   Timing and good distance in front of the boat are the keys.

Fig 88   The spinnaker is hoisted and the crew can now put the spinnaker pole on the guy and mast.

This requires good coordination and timing by the helm and crew. Once the sail is hoisted the crew attaches the spinnaker pole to the guy and attaches the pole to the mast. If the reach is very tight this operation will be hard to perform, so the helm may need to bear away to keep the dinghy upright. The faster you are at this manoeuvre, the quicker you will regain your course and have a chance of laying the mark. It will be a high-pressure boat-handling manoeuvre, so the possibilities of mistakes will also be high. The longer the hoist and set takes, the further you will sail away from your true course and the harder it will be to make the mark. Any action you can take prior to the hoist and bear away will allow shorter hoist times.

You may feel after reading this that the bag system appears to create many handling problems. This is true and the drive towards bags has come from experienced sailors who do not have the boat-handling problems. The bags also have advantages in that they allow weight saving. The weight of the glassfibre spinnaker-chute moulding adds to the weight of the boat and is positioned in the bow, which increases the pitching of the boat. It has been proved that this will slow a boat in choppy conditions. Like many areas it is a question of compromise between ease of handling and performance. If you are good at the boat handling, go for the performance advantage. If the boat handling is a weak area, then go for the system that should give you fewer mistakes. Bags also give the spinnakers a longer life as the constant retrieval by pulling on the retrieval line does wear out the spinnaker in this area. Boats like the Laser 4000, ISO, and RS400 all have chute systems and, because they are all strict one-designs, everybody has to use this system. In fact the systems are now quite sophisticated with the Laser 4000 having the simplest, with one halyard launching the pole and spinnaker from a chute.

SPINNAKER POLES, HEIGHTS AND ANGLES

The design of the spinnaker pole is based on the type of ends and the type of control system used. This becomes a matter of personal choice and I would suggest you look at the best boats in your class and base your system on theirs. The choice in ends is between pushing downwards, upwards or sideways onto the mast attachment. The control system of pole height is more complicated so I will not be able to cover it in any detail within this book. Suffice to say that you will need a positive, adjustable system to control height. If your system has shock-cord controlling height, rather than retrieving rope, then I would suggest you look around the dinghy park for ideas.

The major difference in terms of spinnaker handling between the asymmetric and the conventional spinnaker is that the pole is not adjustable. Admittedly on the RS400 and Laser 4000 you can pull the bowsprit to windward to aid deeper running. With the conventional pole, we need to address pole height and angle. The height must be controlled in a positive way with very little movement when subjected to additional loads in a gust. This will necessitate good uphaul and downhaul systems.

You will find that pole height will be set for different conditions depending upon wind strength, rather than point of sailing. In light winds the pole will be at its lowest in drifting conditions and rise as the wind strength increases. As soon as it becomes easy to fly the spinnaker, the pole should be raised – but to what height? The spinnaker luff is again the key to the trim of the sail and pole height. We know that the luff will curl if the sheet is eased slightly. Where the curl originates is the key to pole height, as it should first break in the middle of the luff and progress towards the head and the foot at the same time. If you find that the luff curls at the upper-third of the sail, then your pole height is too low. If the spinnaker luff curls towards the bottom of the sail, then the pole is probably too high.

The other indicator is to look at the flying height of the two clews of the sail. The aim is to have both flying at the same height. If your pole is too low then the leeward clew will be flying much higher than the clew next to the pole. The spinnaker will have taken on a misshapen appearance rather than being symmetrical. In my experience people tend to make the mistake of flying the pole too low and not adjust it radically for drifting conditions.

Finally, I would suggest some means of calibrating the adjustment system so that you can reproduce known settings. A very simple version of this would be having one felt-tip mark on your jib luff at the normal force 2–4 setting. This not only gives you a common setting, but more importantly will act as a visual reminder for the crew to decide whether they need to adjust the pole.

The pole angle is controlled by the position of the guy. Depending upon the system, this may be pre-set by a stopper knot or small ball on the guy or by the guy in a cleat at the shroud. The stopper knot system has become known as 'twinning lines' (or 'twinners'), and allows the pole to be set just off the forestay (5mm when under load) for tight reaches. For any other leg the pole angle is controlled by the guy in the cleat at the shroud. As a guide, set the pole at right angles to the wind. If the pole is set too far aft then the crew will have problems sheeting the spinnaker. The sail will have to be sheeted very hard, sucking the sail into the mainsail and jib. This will cause excessive collapsing and handling problems. Ease the pole forward and the sail will become more stable and you will be able to ease the sheet without the sail collapsing immediately.

If the pole is not pulled aft to be at right angles to the wind, e.g. to 90 degrees of the centre line on a run, then the spinnaker will have problems flying. In order to practise and become familiar with the handling of spinnakers, I would suggest the following routine. Find an environment that is safe and large enough not to be constrained by the banks. This should be appropriate to your ability level. If you are in doubt, book into a sailing school that can offer spinnaker handling. The wind strength should be light enough not to intimidate you, but strong enough to allow ease of flying for the spinnaker. Hoist the spinnaker on a run and, once confident, play with pole height and angle. It is only by learning yourself in a safe environment that you will be able to appreciate all the sail controls and their function. If you have experienced the controls you will remember them and fully understand the variables.

The final difference between asymmetric spinnakers and conventional symmetrical versions is the effect they have on the balance of the boat. Due to the fact that the asymmetric is much further from the boat the balance between upwind and reaching is not as great. Consequently the centreboard or daggerboard does not need to be raised. With conventional boats the board is raised slightly to change the balance of the boat from upwind to downwind mode. Again, all the new generation of boats are relying on fewer controls to extract the maximum performance: they are easier to sail, with less experience needed. The one-design nature also stops the experts from developing techniques or systems that give the more experienced an advantage.

GYBING THE ASYMMETRIC
(Figs 89–95)

Unlike the conventional spinnaker, where we have different gybes depend-
ing on whether we are reaching or running, the asymmetric has one simple gybe. At first our priority will be to move the spinnaker from gybe to gybe. As we progress with our boat handling, we will be concentrating on gybing from trapeze to trapeze, keeping the power on for as long as possible. Each stage can be broken down, with the speed of execution being the only difference between levels of ability. As the best gybes will be accomplished if power can be kept on for as long as is possible, the helm may want to take the spinnaker sheet if the crew is trapezing. This allows the crew to concentrate on their movements, while maximum speed is maintained.

Fig 89   Preparation is important before the gybe. The jib can be sheeted on both tacks prior to entering the gybe.

Fig 90   The helm has taken over the spinnaker sheet allowing the crew to concentrate on movement. Note the jib is double sheeted and how very little rudder movement is needed at this speed.

Fig 91   The spinnaker is still powering the boat into the gybe, the helm controls the sheet.

Fig 92   The helm grabs the mainsheet to swing the boom as the crew looks for the new spinnaker sheet.

Fig 93   The boom crosses with very little load due to the high speed of the boat. The helm has dropped the old sheet and the crew is already sheeting the new spinnaker sheet. (Boat speed is the key.)

Fig 94   The spinnaker is about to refill, the sheet will have been over-sheeted
to achieve this and will need to be eased as soon as the spinnaker fills.

Fig 95   Starting to power up after the gybe. As the apparent wind increases
the boat will travel faster and the crew will be able to sail lower.

CONVENTIONAL SPINNAKER GYBE *(Figs 96–108)*

As mentioned, you will need to develop two distinct gybes, depending on whether you are reach-to-reach gybing or run-to-run gybing. You may also want to revert back to the reach-to-reach system in conditions which are too windy for the running gybe as it will give the helm more control.

Fig 96   Reach-to-reach gybe on a conventional boat. The helm starts to instigate the gybe with the boat very upright.

Fig 97   The helm concentrates on steering while the crew squares the pole aft.

Fig 98   As the boom comes across, the helm starts to compensate on the rudder and the crew will pull on the windward twinner after releasing the old twinner.

Fig 99   Weight on the windward side followed by the crew starting the changing of the pole. The helm balances the boat with the mainsheet.

Fig 100   The helm trims the new spinnaker sheet while the crew pushes out
the pole. This action is easier if you aim out and then forward.

Fig 101   The crew places the pole onto the mast and can now take the sheet from the helm.

Fig 102   Run-to-run gybes. The crew pulls the pole aft as the helm moves into the middle of the boat.

Fig 103   The helm steers the boat with his knees as the crew transfers the sheet and guy to the helm.

Fig 104   The spinnaker is still flying and the crew pulls the boom over in mid-gybe.

Fig 105   The helm attempts to keep the spinnaker flying while the crew puts the new guy onto the pole.

Fig 106   The crew continues to change the pole as the helm flies the spinnaker.

Fig 107   The crew has just started to take the guy and sheet back from the helm as they settle down on the new gybe.

'Do not be afraid to sail higher to give you the speed and the apparent wind to drive low. Just remember, what goes up must come down!'

Ian Walker, International 14 World Champion and IYRU World Champion (470 double handed)

Fig 108   Ian Walker, 1994 IYRU World Champion (double handed) and past International 14 World Champion.

10

The Rig

The driving force of the boat, whether it is a singlehander or a twin trapeze, new generation dinghy with racks and asymmetric, is the rig. It can appear complicated, but do not be put off because as you start to understand the various options you will soon be able to make decisions on the rig. So what is the rig? I will deal with the mast and sails and how we can vary certain positions for different wind strengths to make the parts work in a more integrated manner. The rig we will consider has both main and jib and is set on a mast with a single set of adjustable spreaders. If you sail a Laser you have no option in mast settings, although you may still adjust parts of your rig based on the ideas put forward in this chapter.

It is well worth remembering that the fine tuning of a rig can be carried out by the sail controls mentioned in Chapter 5. In terms of major tuning though, what options do we have?

1. Mast rake.
2. Rig tension.
3. Spreader length.
4. Spreader angle.

The actual section specification for the mast may be one-design and controlled by the manufacturer. However, even in the new generation of manufacturers' one-designs, competitors can still normally adjust the four options listed above. The important aspect to remember is that the four options will all affect each other. If we increase the mast rake, then this will affect the rig tension if we still pull the rig tension adjuster to the same mark.

HOW TO MEASURE THE FOUR AREAS

It is important to check via your class newsletter or tuning guide exactly how each class takes its measurement. I will give you some broad ideas but you must check the class-specific way. This information can come from fellow sailors or from the multitude of tuning booklets that are now in circulation.

Mast Rake

Mast rake is generally measured by a tape measure attached to the main halyard and hoisting it to the top of the mast. To have a consistent measurement each time we must always hoist it to the same mark that we would do for the mainsail. The tape is then pulled tight and a central measurement point is used. On some classes this will be the top of the transom and on other classes it will be the intersection of floor and transom. The sailmaker or class tuning guide will give you this specific detail.

Mast rake can be varied by use of more or less rig tension, a common adjustment while sailing, or by changing the shroud lengths by using the adjusters where the shrouds are attached to the boat. Certain classes will use fast pins (or a similar product) to allow the change in length to be done on the water. This change can only be carried out with the rig tension totally let off and is for advanced sailors only.

Rig Tension *(Fig 109)*

As already mentioned, this can change the rake of the dinghy and is probably the most useful control that we have. Again the key to measurement is consistency so that we can use the figures for comparisons. In order to measure the rig tension we will need a rig tension meter. Available from most well-equipped dinghy chandlers, there are two main brands (Superspars and Loos), which unfortunately are calibrated to a different numerical system. Both systems are very similar in how they work, hooking over the shroud or jib wire. They are then pulled back to a set mark and the deflection point of the wire is noted. To ensure consistency, always use only the jib or shroud and measure at the same point above the deck. The reading will be influenced by the thickness of wire and tension, with the jib having a lower reading than the shrouds for the same wire diameter. As long as you are measuring the same stay as your guide and with the same diameter wire then you can compare your rig tension with the class tuning guide. Rig tension not only affects the rake but will also change the fullness and power of the jib. The mast bend will also be affected by the combination of rig tension and spreader deflection.

Spreader Length *(Fig 110)*

The spreaders act as struts to help keep the mast upright in our boats. The length of the spreaders will affect how much our mast bends, since an increase in rig tension will force the mast forwards creating bend, as the spreaders are forced by the shrouds trying to form a straight line with no spreader deflection. Due to this fact the length of the spreaders is critical. To measure the length, place a tape measure on the side of the mast and measure to the intersection of the spreader and shroud, ignoring any spreader cover beyond the shroud. It is imperative that both spreaders are the same, exact length. If not, then the forces will not be even on both sides of the mast and we will have different bend characteristics on both tacks.

Spreader Angle *(Fig 111)*

We have two ways of changing the spreader angle. Either move the shroud base in relation to the spreader, or adjust the spreader angle at the spreader root with an adjuster. The second system is by far the simplest and most popular system, with all mast manufacturers offering some adjustable system. The easiest way of measuring spreader deflection is to place a sail batten across the spreaders and then measure from the batten edge, resting against the shrouds, to the aft face of the mast. Again compare this with the class tuning sheet.

This can all become very complicated, so my aim is to keep it as simple and as successful as possible. For the majority of us, having the same speed as the current champion will be adequate, so let us use his/her settings. You know how

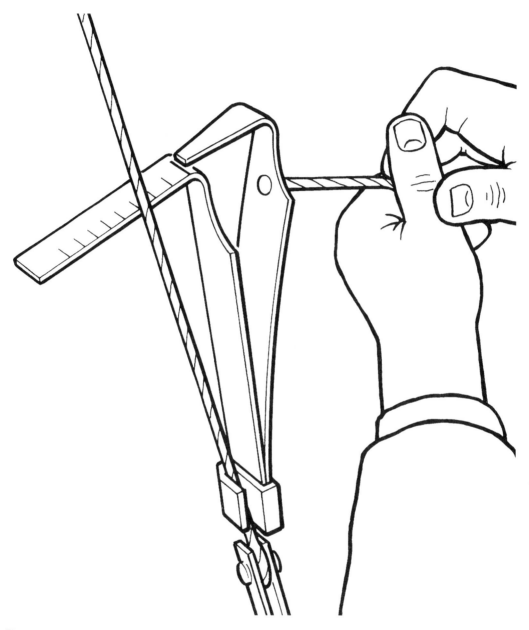

Fig 109   A Loos tension meter being applied to a shroud. The scale is read
against the resting position of the shroud.

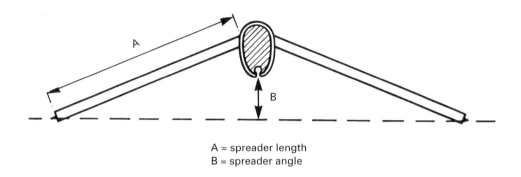

A = spreader length
B = spreader angle

Fig 110   Measuring the spreader length and deflection.

to measure the four major variables, so set your boat up in an identical fashion.

RIG-SETTING

As well as setting your boat up in an identical way to the tuning guide, you should also understand some of the effects of tuning for different wind conditions. For a complete guide I have suggested some sources for further reading in Chapter 14. In basic terms I think that the rig needs two settings, these being powerful or depowered. We need the depowered setting for very light conditions, as well as windy conditions, with very slight differences between them. For the rest of the time we will use the powerful rig as we search for the maximum drive possible. Then, as we become over-powered, as the wind builds, we can revert to our depowered settings. It may sound complicated, but there are some simple rules that we can stick to.

The Powerful Rig

The powerful rig is designed to generate maximum power. To achieve this we want the sails at their fullest, which can be done by having the rake as upright as possible within our tuning guidelines. The spreaders will have been swung forward at the adjusters to give as straight a mast as is possible. The rig tension will probably be medium, stopping the jib luff from sagging, but not forcing the spreaders to bend the mast.

As we become over-powered we will want to rake the rig as this will allow greater twisting of the sails, as well as reducing the height of the rig. More importantly as we are being over-powered we will rake the centreboard aft and the rig will also be raked to stay balanced with the centreboard. If we cannot rake the daggerboard, as in a Laser 4000, then we can create twist in the mainsail by using the cunningham. This

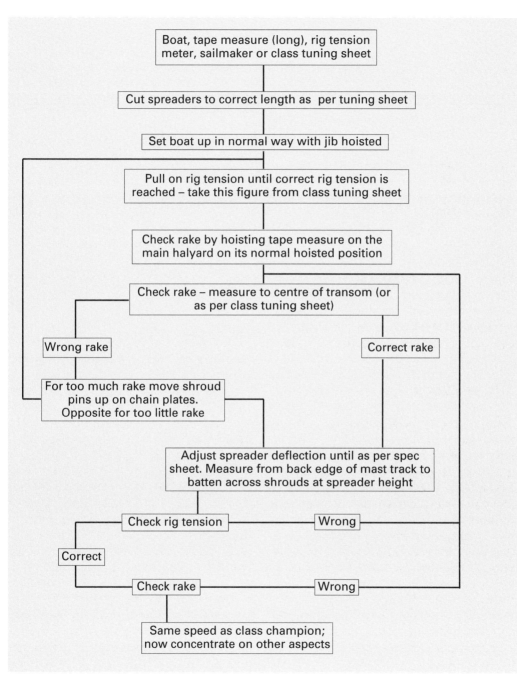

Fig 111   Follow the flow chart to tune your dinghy.

will blade out the main (flatten), as well as twist off the head of the sail and depower the rig.

The Depowered Rig

If we know that the wind is going to be strong, we can set the rig up in the dinghy park to give us an advantage. Rake will be crucial, so go to the aft-setting on the tuning guide. This will probably be achieved by adjusting the shroud lengths at the shroud adjusters. Go down on the adjusters to shorten the shrouds. Pull on the rig tension and check this. We will probably be looking for a similar rig tension to other conditions but with more rake. If we had just eased off on the rig tension to increase rake without changing the shroud length, then our jib would be too powerful due to the lack of rig tension. We will also flatten the mainsail by trying to allow the mast to bend. This can be done at deck level by allowing the mast to move forward and at spreader height by swinging the spreaders aft.

All of these depowering strategies will also be used in light winds with the exception of rake, where we should be as upright as possible. It sounds complicated but it's not as long as you look at the class tuning guide and talk to other sailors. The other action that you need to take is to rig your boat and run through all of these settings, using markings so that you will be able to reproduce the settings. Write on the boat with felt-tip pens so that it is easy to find the correct settings. Draw on the

Symmetrical Boats are Fast
Finally on the subject of tuning we need to look at some simple measurements that will make sure that your boat is symmetrical in set-up and hence fast.

1. Look up the track of your mast to check if the mast is straight sideways in the boat. If it is not, check that the spreaders are the same length, same angle and acting at the same height on the shroud. Sometimes they slip down on the shrouds as they need to bear at right angles to the shroud. Simply push them up if they have slipped down.
2. A simple way of checking the spreader angle is by measuring to each spreader tip from the centre of the transom. If this measurement is not the same on both sides then run through the checks on length and deflection.

mast by the spreaders, to show which way to turn the adjusters when you are making changes. Finally go on race-training days run by your class association, as it is here that the very specific knowledge to your class will be passed on by the coaches within that class. All classes have their subtle differences. For example, the singlehanders with adjustable rake tend to go more upright as the wind increases to allow more leech tension, while the jib and mainsail boats go for more rake.

11
The Race

Sailing dinghies in itself is a very rewarding pastime, but racing will allow you to look at physical, mental and tactical elements that combine to make sailing one of the great all-round sports.

PREPARATION

Dinghy racing is a combination of:

Technical skills – how we sail the boat and set it up.
Physical skills – the physical attributes to sail each particular dinghy.
Mental skills – how we use our experience to make decisions on the race course.

Obviously there is some overlap between these areas. What I am interested in is how much we can learn without direct experience and what can be decided prior to getting on the race course. In this chapter we are going to explore these areas and look at a typical club race. This will allow you to experience a race from the comfort of your armchair, still learning valuable lessons.

It is important that we appreciate that a high percentage of our performance can come from sound preparation. Much of this will be derived from clear evaluation and goal-setting to allow realistic targets to be met. In order to enter your first club race you should be proficient in tacking and gybing, and understand the feedback from the sails to produce good straight line speed. Above all you should *want* to race and have the confidence to take part. I am sure that wherever you sail, you will find much encouragement from fellow club members. Hopefully someone within the club, be they training officer, class captain or race trainer, will guide you through the specific knowledge that you need at that club. Apart from this basic boat handling, you need to understand some simple rules.

The first area to start with is you, whether you are a crew or a helm. It is important that you have the correct sailing gear to keep you warm and safe. Chapter 3 has addressed this, though I would recommend that even if the club allows racing in certain conditions without a buoyancy aid that you still wear one. Once you yourself are properly equipped you need to make sure that the boat is properly equipped. Certain boats will require a buoyancy check, although this is less important with the modern designs. Often you will be able to check this with a simple pressure check on the internal buoyancy. What you will need in order to race is insurance so it is worth checking your insurance to see if any clauses on racing are included. The club will insist that the insurance is to a minimum third-party value, though the figure will depend upon the club and the country.

Your final preparation for the boat is to calibrate anything that moves. Often in the excitement of a race where we are trying to perform activities in a hurry we can very easily make a mistake. Preparation is all about trying to ensure that there are as few mistakes as possible. We are all going to make mistakes, but the fewer we make the quicker we will sail around the course. Items such as spinnaker halyards can be marked with a water-resistant felt-tip pen. Mark the halyard where you can see the mark, just as you pull it to the correct position at the cleat. It is all too easy in a race to leave the halyard 25cm short of its correct position. The spinnaker will be hard to fill and you will be surprised just how long it will take for you to discover this mistake. Mark the halyard and you know that the spinnaker is hoisted all the way. Other sheets can be marked, e.g. the jib sheets in their normal position. This will allow the crew to pull them to the average position every tack without looking at the jib. They may not have the specific knowledge to look at the jib and make a decision on trimming. The mark will also aid communication between helm and crew. How often as a crew have I been told, when easing the jib, 'No, not that much!'

With both crew and boat ready for the race, you need to be aware that the race will be controlled by the International Yacht Racing Union, IYRU racing rules and also the local sailing instructions. Apart from the rules which many books cover, the main points that you will need to know are the course and how to start. I strongly advise that you take your time over your first race, deciding what you are going to do before going on the water. Set a goal of completing the race and enjoying yourself, do not put pressure on yourself for results. Allow plenty of time to rig your boat and sail out to the race area, even allowing for a sticking halyard or a queue on the launching ramp. Prior to going on the water you may want to write a few notes on your boat. In order to do this stick a piece of white fablon on your boat and then write on it with your water-resistant felt-tip pen. The start sequence and the course are probably the most complex areas that you will need to remember.

Courses can vary from club to club, as will the start line. I have already described the changes that are going on in courses. The conventional triangular 'Olympic course', as used in the Olympics of 1992, has been replaced by an 'Olympic trapezoid' square course, which incorporates more windward-leeward sailing. The course is still very much in an evolutionary stage and the courses at clubs may reflect the personal preferences of sailors within the club or the constraints imposed by the shape of the water. Suffice to say that you need to remember which marks to go around and which side, starboard or port. I think that it is worth running through the course with your crew. You may also wish to decide how you will approach each part of the course. At all times the way that you sail the course should be designed to put as little pressure as possible on your boat handling. If you are approaching a mark where you will round it to port and then bear away on to a run, decide that approaching on starboard is the best option. Then you are the right-of-way boat and can sort yourself out prior to bearing away. If you approach on port, you will have to watch for other boats, as well as tack and immediately bear away, a complex manoeuvre for even the best boat handlers. Make your life as easy as possible. Often the best sailors make it look all very simple and under control, because that is exactly how they have planned the approach.

The start line and the starting sequence will be fully explained within the sailing instructions, which will vary from club to club. In the past few years the courses have been experimented with and so too has the start sequence. The traditional way was to have a ten-minute warning signal (flag and sound signal), followed by a five-minute signal, and then five minutes later, the start. This ten-minute sequence has now been reduced by many clubs and classes to 6 / 3 / start as the extra four minutes is not actually needed in the small fleet racing of the 1990s. The trend is also for more, shorter races, so with three races a day the start sequence is important. For larger fleets the ten-minute sequence may still be applicable. There is a lot to do within this six-minute sequence, so you will need to be organized. For more advanced starting, I talk about logical pre-planned sequences in Chapter 13. In your first few races the goal should be to understand the signals and the position of the line, hopefully putting your boat where you want to at the correct time.

Starting is an important skill and involves many areas. Prior to the start we can plan a strategy for the first beat. This may be influenced by tide or the close proximity of a shore line or a wind bend (more on this later). Our starting strategy will reflect this. We also need good slow boat handling to allow us to position our boat at the right position. We will also need good spatial awareness to know where the start line is. The start line may be between a boat and a mark, a pole on the land and a mark, or may even be a transit from two poles on the shore line. The important thing to know is where you are in relation to the line.

A useful tool employed by sailors of all ability levels is the use of a transit, which is particularly useful for starting in the middle of a line as we do not have the reference of the buoy or boat in the water. It is also very good in tidal situations where the entire fleet may make a mistake in judging its position due to the tidal stream. By looking at your position in relation to the shore rather the fleet you will be aware of your position in relation to the start line and not the fleet.

Information on the tide will also make our starting easier to control. If we know that the tide will be taking us towards the

Simple Starting Rules
• Set realistic goals.
• Learn to stop the boat and move off as a means of controlling speed.
• Do not sail too far away from the line because the wind may drop.
Start on starboard as often as possible.
• Read the sailing instructions and understand the course, start sequence and the following flags: class flag; preparatory flag; recall flag; abandonment flag.
• One day we will have a simpler system, but until that day arrives you will save a lot of time and worry by understanding the flags that control the racing.

line, then we should be aware that this will make it harder starting at the starboard end. Conversely if the tide is against us, then starting at the port end will be harder and just getting on to the line will be the number one priority.

ADVANCED STARTING

As we move up the competition ladder the importance of the start becomes fundamental. The new-style races are shorter and the start is deciding more of the race. We have smaller fleets and less general recalls with the emphasis on picking out premature starters rather than having another restart. Excellent close-quarter boat-handling skills are an essential part of putting you in the correct spot. I also think it imperative that you dominate the start. The best starters are all confident of their ability and make it clear to all around them that they are going to get a good start. You can be positive and dominant by your actions rather than your words. Imagine a leeward-end start. The wind may be slightly biased to this end, or there may be a tide advantage out on this left side of the course, so you want to win the start from this end. The ideal position will be buoy-end with control of the boat that is to windward of you. In order to maintain control it is important that you are tightly positioned underneath this boat so that they will not be able to dictate the start. This will be dictated by you: if you want to foot you can and if you want to pinch you can. Also in terms of acceleration on the start line you can bear away to create space for acceleration while this boat cannot.

In terms of skills you will find that you need the following: the ability to tack from a standstill and then tack back with no acceleration; and the ability to stay in one position almost head to wind without tacking. These can be practised next to any mark on the water. Simply try to stay next to the buoy. As you drift away try to tack with no speed and no acceleration. The tacking is perfected by using roll as a means of steering and careful positioning of crew weight. You may also need to back the jib to knock the bow around, which will require close communication between helm and crew. At its best, you both will know what to do without speaking.

The staying still, holding position is a more difficult skill and more controversial, due to the fact that you will need to row with the rudder. Our rules' advisers say that as no speed is being generated and the rudder does not cross the centreline of the boat this is not sculling. Place the boat head to wind. In order to keep it here you will need to row repeatedly on one side of the centreline, e.g. if the bow is always trying to tack, you will need to have the tiller in the starboard side of the boat, constantly trying to pull the bow back to the left. Practise this away from starts as you will spend some time tacking and also going into 'irons'. Only use this skill when you feel confident that it will work on a crowded start line.

Meanwhile at the leeward-end of the start line we are trying to engineer our start. Our best position is underneath the windward boat. By having the ability to slow down, head to wind, we can control the windward boat. If that boat tacks away we must perform our double tack to regain our preferred position underneath his bow. If this boat is also fighting for the best start, they may try to get around the back of you and underneath your boat in the preferred position. As they do this you must also accelerate down the line maintaining the dominant position. If they do take the dominant position you can use reversing skills to reverse out and try to win it back as they have now become the windward boat and so are in a weaker position. (In using the rules to your advantage it is important that you are very confident in your knowledge.) All this manoeuvring is a battle of wits, a tactical game of chess, using boat-handling skills and confidence to take a risk.

We will all make mistakes in these positions and some of the skill of dinghy racing is recognizing these mistakes early enough. If we are trying to start at the leeward end and we are early, then an alternative plan can be used. If you are early it is pointless waiting for the start; nothing is going to change. If you start to rectify the mistake with 10–15 seconds before the start, then you may still make a good start from the favoured end. The alternative plan should also have been discussed prior to the start by helm and crew. If you are going to start on port and duck the odd boat, who is going to call the boats, who will make decisions on tacking and ducking boats?

Starting skills can rapidly be improved by the setting of realistic goals and careful evaluation afterwards. This may involve a coach or instructor who will be able to act not only as another pair of eyes but also as an unbiased observer. So often we do not use others within our sport, while other sports use outside help frequently. If we want to learn golf, we are taught the basics and then use a coach to progress. At present this is not the case within dinghy sailing, but hopefully this will change, with the result that we improve and reach our own individual goals more quickly. Books and videos, as well as watching good practice, can help to improve your starting. For those new to racing I would recommend: *Capture the Wind*, a video available from the RYA. For those more advanced I would recommend *Winning in One Designs* by Dave Perry and *The North U Smart Course* (either the course or booklet) available from North Sails.

RULES

Before starting your first race you will need to know a limited number of rules. The rule book itself looks a little daunting, but the rules themselves are there to cover every eventuality, and in your first race you will only need to understand six. You will be pleased to know that the administrators of our sport are reviewing the rules to try and make them simpler and easier to understand. The six scenarios that we need to be aware of are as follows:

Port/Starboard
Windward/leeward
Overtaking
Tacking/gybing
Mark rounding
What to do after a mistake

Run over these scenarios with another club sailor before your first race or alternatively read some of the excellent books on the sailing rules.

SHIFTS OR BENDS – THE KEY TO UPWIND SAILING *(Fig 112)*

As sailing is one of the most 'open' sports, experience is worth a great deal. The specific experience of being able to recognize the difference between a shift and a bend is crucial. The reason for this is that the decision we take is dependent on what type of shifting wind we are sailing in. If we are lifted in a shifting wind we will stay on that tack, but if we are lifted in a wind bend then we will probably tack.

Again preparation is a crucial area. This will give us a forecast and an indication of how the wind will be affected by the surrounding land, and we can also track the wind once we are on the race course. Prior to the start this can be carried out with the use of a compass: simply point the boat head to wind and read the wind bearing that is indicated. Again it may be useful to write this down with the water-resistant felt-tip pen. Alternatively you can read the wind from each tack. Note your heading while sailing along and write this down, then tack and repeat the operation on the other tack. After carrying this out for a minimum of twenty minutes you will start to build up a picture of what the wind is doing.

Beware, though, as this is the past and you should always be on the look-out for changes in the weather as the race progresses. You may have to force yourself to look upwind and at the other boats. No doubt you will lose a little speed in doing this but it is very important as we sail in the *now* and not in the past. The past just gives us more information on where to look in the 'present'. So what are we looking for? We need to know about changes in wind velocity, gusts coming down the race course and also shifts in the wind direction. In terms of the latter, we are constantly trying to decide if the wind is shifting or is part of a permanent bend. Returning to our boat sailing upwind, let us assume that the wind is shifting either side of a mean wind. Then for a given tack we will either be sailing on the mean or we will be lifted or headed depending upon which side of the mean the wind is. If we are lifted on starboard, then if we tack we will be headed. Consequently in a shifting wind the person who manages to arrive at the windward mark, having only sailed on lifts, will be leading. I say arrive at the windward mark, as often you do need to compromise and sail some of the beat on the mean or headed in order to get to the windward mark.

The wind bend diagram shows the wind is normally progressing in one direction, perhaps due to the effect of land, a headland or the arrival of a new wind, for example a sea breeze. Whatever the reason, we need to be aware that only one tack will be the paying tack as long as this trend continues. We now have to decide how far the wind is going to shift as this will help in the decision of how far to tack into the bend. In effect it is like running around a bend on an athletics track. If we are in lane 1, we will sail less distance than the sailor in lane 8. Again we have the problem of arriving at the windward mark: there is no point in being in lane 1 if lane 3 would have been enough. Due to the progressive nature of the shift some of the sailing will need to take place on the headed tack. This will allow us to get to the correct inside position.

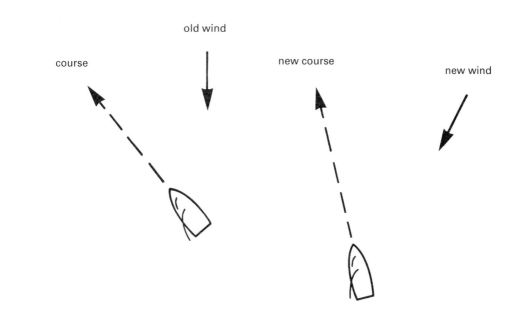

Fig 112(a) A new wind that shifts permanently to the right will lift us on starboard.

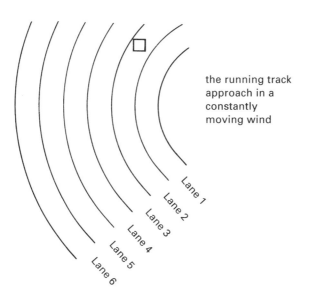

the running track approach in a constantly moving wind

Fig 112 (b) If the wind is constantly shifting one way, we need to decide which of the running track lanes will take us to the mark.

LAY LINES *(Fig 113)*

If the race course is the chess board that our tactical battle takes place on, then the edge of the board on the upwind leg is the lay line. Once you are on the lay line, then by sailing upwind at your most efficient you will arrive at the windward mark. Obviously as the wind shifts then your lay line will change. If the wind lifts you will need to free off to reach the mark, if it heads you then you will sail to the mark on a header and still have to tack for the mark. The lay lines should be avoided at all costs, unless you decide to be extreme on one side of the course. As long as you are not on a lay line, then your options will still be open. As soon as you are on a lay line your options are determined and the wind will decide if you sail all the way on a lift or a header.

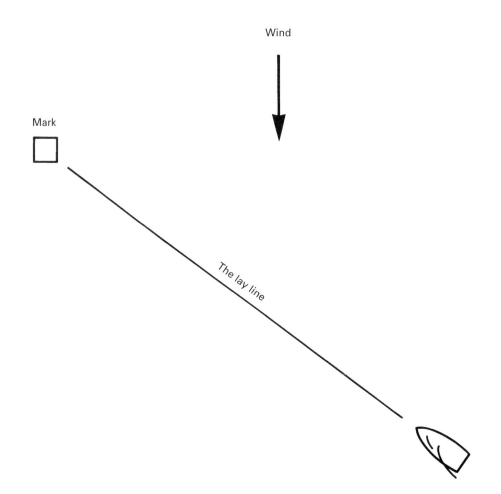

Fig 113   On the lay line. If the wind shifts to the right we overstand. If it shifts to the left we have to sail all the way to the mark on a header.

'Boat-handling skills will create the gap to leeward, allowing you consistently to start well. The real skill is the timing of the gap creation, with observation and experience providing the key to truly successful starting.'

John Merricks, IYRU World Champion and 1994 420 World Champion

Fig 114   John Merricks, 1994 IYRU World Champion (double handed) and 1994 420 World Champion.

113

12

Fitness, Food, Water and Sun

Health and lifestyles are constantly being evaluated by modern society. Dinghy sailing provides us with a unique, environmentally friendly sport that will keep us in all-round physical shape. Obviously the extent to which this is true will depend upon which dinghy you are sailing and what the predominant conditions are. In order to enjoy our sport to the full we will need to be aware of fitness and lifestyle issues.

So how fit do you need to be to enjoy sailing? The answer is very much dependent upon the type of dinghy and your competitive aspirations. I look at the performance profile in the next chapter and this will allow you to define the physical parameters for each type of boat. Compared to many sports, you do not need an extreme level of fitness, certainly in aerobic terms. Very rarely will you be out of breath due to physical exertion. Because of the very open nature of our sport, experience, tactics, strategy and technically setting the boat up correctly will give us the speed, rather than this being obtained solely from physical fitness. Sailing fitness is not extreme and good all-over body conditioning will result from sailing. This should be maintained out of season (if you stop sailing for some of the winter months), such as by

rowing on one of the many brands of rowing machines, designed for gyms, health clubs and the home. I have found the Concept 2 ergometer the best, with excellent build quality, combined with clear information on your performance. No video screens or gadgets, it just gives you your output in watts, calories burned or pace. Other information will give you your rowing-stroke rate, with new models giving the option of displaying your heart rate. This is transmitted from a sophisticated elastic strap around your chest and will provide the clearest target for any training programme.

The saying 'No pain, no gain' has probably caused more injuries and more over-training than any other saying! To exercise correctly for sailing I would recommend training at 60–70 per cent of your maximum heart rate. As a rough guide, your maximum heart rate is calculated by taking your age from 220 e.g. a 30-year-old is 220–30 = 190. The training band will be 60–70 per cent of this, which is 114–133. By training on a rowing machine at this intensity we will develop all-over conditioning as well as building a large aerobic base for our sailing. Over a period of time the duration should be built up to at least thirty minutes per session with exercise taking place a

114

Fig 115   The Concept 2 Model c rowing machine, the best rowing ergometer.

minimum of three times a week to give the desired result. Specific guidance should be taken from the instructors at your training venue. If you have any doubts from a health viewpoint about embarking on additional fitness for your sailing, then you should consult your doctor before beginning.

Exercise can only be sustained by correct fuel within our bodies, and this will

115

come from eating correctly. Unfortunately the Western world does not have a very good track record in terms of healthy eating. Too many people are overweight, with the majority of men and women eating too much fat and not enough fibre. Sailing, whether racing or cruising, can go on for many hours and to sustain this we need to try to eat approximately 60 per cent of our diet as carbohydrates while cutting down the amount of fat that we consume (targets of less than 25–30 per cent fat are being cited by governments). In order to do this we need to know what foods contain carbohydrate, fat and fibre.

Unfortunately, this is not that easy as most foods contain mixtures of all of these substances. If we consider dinghy sailing, I would advise a good breakfast with sensible snacks while out sailing, and then concentrate your main meal on dishes which will include potatoes, rice, pasta or bread. These foods all contain large amounts of carbohydrate and are low fat. We consume a lot of fat by either spreading it on our bread or cooking foods in fat. By simply stopping eating fried foods or reducing our intake we can have a significant impact on the quantity of fat that we consume. The traditional English fried breakfast contains large quantities of fat with fried bread being a leading example. Many families have replaced this traditional breakfast with muesli and other cereals. These are frequently high fibre and carbohydrate-based foods. In order to check the percentage of fat in your food, simply look at the nutritional label on the box and multiply the number of grammes of fat by ten, and divide by the total number of calories (Kcal), multiplying by 100 to give the approximate answer. Sainsbury's raisin Bran (1995) has 0.6g of fat per serving. Total calories (Kcal) per serving are 98. The relationship is 6 divided by 98 = 0.06 × 100 = 6% fat, easily inside the government targets. This is a very approximate system, but will give you a guide as to which products to eat.

Snacks during the day, or while out sailing, will frequently be designed around ease of eating and their ability to be carried on board the boat. Fruit is good, but provides on the whole very little energy, though bananas are high-energy foods (with their own built-in packaging!) and raisins also provide strong supplies of energy. Sandwiches are also very good, particularly brown or grain bread (wholemeal, granary, and so on). Be careful of the fillings as large quantities of butter, cheese and mayonnaise will send your fat intake for the day upwards. Try using the low-fat spreads or low-fat cheese if you go for this option. Meats like turkey are now easily available in sliced form, giving low-fat alternatives. The traditional snack of chocolate bars are very easy to carry on dinghies, but unfortunately are normally over our fat guidelines. Certain brands are now available that will give you quality energy from carbohydrate in a conventional chocolate bar form, such as Maxim bars and Power bars, available in various flavours. The best rule for any nutritional help is that the diet should be balanced, making sure that correct amounts of carbohydrate, fat, protein, minerals and vitamins are eaten. More and more information is now available for the general public, so you should be able to follow a diet suitable for dinghy sailing.

There is one substance that as dinghy sailors we should be very aware of: water, not for sailing on, but for drinking while we are enjoying our sport. As dinghy sailors we have to be aware of dehydration, since our protective clothing and the fact that we can be out in the elements for many hours makes us vulnerable. A warm day, safely protected from the elements by our dry suit or wet suit, are the conditions in which we will need to drink to replenish our water supplies. The problem with dehydration is that you are not aware that it is happening, you just realize at the end of the day that it was a long time since you went to the toilet! In order to make sure that we do not dehydrate it is important to take water out on the race course. This can easily be carried in small, plastic water bottles or in one of the many cycling drinking bottles that are on the market. If you do use reusable drinking bottles it is important that you keep them in a clean healthy state. To achieve this, have a separate bottle for each person on board to avoid spreading germs. You should also sterilize the bottles each evening with some of the babies' bottles' sterilising solutions, which are available from any supermarket. If you have water on board, then also make sure that you drink as you go around the course, particularly in light, hot conditions. It is proven scientifically that as you start to dehydrate your decision-making effectiveness decreases as well as your athletic performance and concentration, all key skills in modern dinghy sailing, whether you are simply sailing for fun or concentrating on a race.

The final area that we need to be aware of to maximize our enjoyment is the sun. It seems ironic that the sun beating down on our face can now be the enemy. The great freedom that we have in sailing and competing against the elements is now becoming a threat if we do not take the correct protection. Due to the effect of pollution and chemicals altering the ozone layer, the power of the sun is now a problem worldwide and not just a southern hemisphere problem. We need to protect our skin and eyes against the sun. Both are at risk as the sun's rays are reflected from the water and sails onto our bodies. The worst scenario is that you may develop skin cancer – after all large numbers of Australians now treat having skin cancers removed as a normal operation. Children are the most vulnerable, so everything possible should be done to make sure that they are never burnt by the sun. You are most at risk if you burn easily which usually means blue-eyed, freckly, fair-skinned people. However, the ability to tan is no guarantee that you are not putting your skin at risk.

The use of long-sleeved shirts and light clothing combined with a hat is a good base. All non-clothed areas should be protected by total-block or high-factor sun screens (20+). The numerical figure refers to the additional protection that you will be applying. If you burn in 15 minutes without the screen, then this added protection will give you 15 × 20 = 300 minutes, or 6 hours. Brands such as Riemann P20 and Tan Ban should help in the fight against ultraviolet rays.

With sunglasses you need to buy a pair that will take out 100 per cent ultraviolet light as well as blue light and ultraviolet radiation. Check the manufacturers' specification in this area as some glasses will actually do more harm than good. The leading brands such as Oakley, Vuarnet and Bolle should have a style that will give large wrap-around protection as well as making you look the part! If you are worried by any marks on your skin, particularly moles or changing, irregular shapes, then consult your doctor.

13
Where From Here?

The key question at the end of this book is, 'where to now'? Not surprisingly the answer will be different for us all, but I feel that there are some common issues to be addressed by everyone. Certain chapters within this book will hold some of the answers, so I hope that you will revisit those chapters to add to your skill levels or to check the sequence running through a manoeuvre. I believe that the common issue is how we wish to improve. By improving our skills we will be able to enjoy the sport of dinghy sailing to its potential by sailing in more varied conditions, by taxing ourselves physically, mentally and technically and by simply getting more fun out of the sport. I do not see this practice as result-orientated for the reasons I listed in Chapter 4. The outcome (result) should improve but all we can actually control are the various processes.

PERFORMANCE PROFILE

In order for us to consider the process I think it appropriate that we conclude this book with a look at the performance profile. This has been developed in numerous sports, originally at elite level to aid identification of areas that require improving. (Much of this work was carried out by Butler and Hardy and Loughborough University.) I have successfully developed it with in sailing with the help of Ian Maynard, sports psychologist to the British Olympic Sailing Team. Much of this work was carried out with Nigel Buckley and Pete Newlands, 1988 470 World Champions.

The premise of the Performance Profile is that the profile is specific to individuals. It should reflect the specific elements of their sport and their level within that sport. Therefore it is pointless using the Buckley/Newlands profile as their profile reflects Olympic two-man dinghy competition. The other advantage of a specific profile is that because you have designed it you will have a high degree of responsibility for the action it recommends. In this way evaluation and improvements are likely to take place. Improvements in most fields will come about by training, followed by competition or action with a period of evaluation after the action. This period of evaluation will be crucial to structuring the next period of training which will lead to further improvements. The training, the action and the evaluation will all need to be specific to the needs of the individual.

The Performance Profile revolves around a number of key stages:
1. Identification of elements that make up your sport.
2. Weighting given to these elements by allocating their importance.
3. Evaluation of your last performance.

4. Calculation of which areas to concentrate your training on.

In order to consider this I will use a number of examples. We will first consider the single-handed sailor at club level. He or she will be a Laser sailor, and we will divide the profile into the following areas: technical, tactical, strategic and sailing. We will now consider what elements may be placed within each of these four areas.

Technical

Sailing a Laser is a lower priority area than sailing a 470. The 470 rules allow technical developments with choice of mast, sails, foils, layout, and so on. In fact most new classes tend to follow the Laser concept and opt for the manufacturers' one-design. As we have no choice in these areas the only aspect we need to consider is preparation.

Once we have identified the areas, we need to allocate a score of 1–10, reflecting the area's relative importance. We may therefore decide that the sail is one area we need to address, giving it a score of 7. The condition of the hull may also be an issue, as may be the finish on the daggerboard.

Tactical

This area should contain elements that allow us to make decisions, for example the rules, the sailing instructions or our knowledge in terms of covering, herding, and so on.

Strategic

This area should contain information that will allow us to plan strategies before the race, such as weather forecasts and details of currents, tides and local conditions. If sailing on a particular piece of water where conditions are unstable then one sailor normally emerges at the front of the fleet due to the strength of his local knowledge. The more unstable the piece of water the more importance should be placed on acquiring this local knowledge.

Sailing

This will be the largest group in most people's profiles, consisting, as it does, of all the set moves or actions that you will need to acquire. These will include elements such as tacking, gybing (possibly split between reach-to-reach and run-to-run), acceleration, sail-setting, completing 720-degree turns, getting out of 'irons', sitting out and starting. From my experience of Laser sailing I would give the highest weighting to starting, sitting out and acceleration (score 10). Slightly behind these with a score of 9 would be tacking and gybing, as I believe if you start well with good acceleration and can sit out well then these will give better results than for the person who is excellent at tacking and gybing but cannot start. Again the important aspect is that this profile is an evaluation of the sailing of a Laser sailor at club level.

Assessment

Having completed this exercise we have identified areas of importance and given them a weighting from a low priority at 1 progressing to the highest priority at 10. We now consider each of these areas based upon the last time that we sailed, giving our performance a weighting from 1–10. Again if we completed the task with 100 per cent perfection give the task ten, descending down to a poor score at 1. In order for the profile to work we now need to use some simple maths to identify the areas that we will need to concentrate our practice-time upon. The formula is as follows: 10 – your performance score × importance score, e.g. 10 – tacking score of 6 = 4 × importance score of 9 = 36. Having completed this for all areas we look for the highest scores as these are the areas where by investing a little effort in practice we will reap the largest reward in overall performance. This may appear a little complicated but is an ideal example of self-coaching. We are simply analysing our sailing and deciding which areas need improvement. So often I see sailors who do not identify the weak areas of their sailing. They may be very good at boat handling in a force 4 wind. Consequently you normally find them out sailing in this wind and not really addressing the weakness of sailing in light winds, the result being that they make smaller and smaller improvements in the force 4 wind and never improve in light winds.

Goal-setting also needs to be considered, and the goals must be realistic, If you want to be a competent all-round sailor in all conditions then you must address this, rather than specializing in your favourite conditions. The best sailors are normally all-round sailors with no real weakness in certain wind strengths. Discuss your goals with fellow sailors and your club race trainer or instructor so that a plan can be devised to allow improvement in racing, cruising or just getting more fun from the sport.

'IN AN IDEAL WORLD'

The performance profile is just one way of looking at areas in which to improve. Another popular way which allows all members of the team to have input is by constructing an 'in an ideal world plan'. This will say who does what and in what order. It has two benefits:

1. You can decide without the pressure of boat handling what is the ideal order of activities, during a manoeuvre or sailing on a particular leg of a course.
2. This sequence will give you a base for analysis afterwards so that actions or even the sequence can be changed to improve performance.

Again, just like performance profiles, no specific failure is being apportioned, it is simply evaluating a race or activity. So often individuals do not like evaluation because of the allocation of blame. Both these systems try to avoid that allocation as even if the task was not performed as it might be we are trying to identify new training plans, to remedy the situation rather than allocate blame. The following was designed by Mark Chisnell and his crew Paul Constable during their 470 campaign. The entire race was 'sailed' on dry land, deciding how they would carry out manoeuvres and also what information and action was needed on a certain leg of the course. This is designed around sailing to windward.

This system allows the helm to concentrate on speed while still receiving the information that will allow the helm and crew to make tactical decisions. As the courses that we race on have

Crew Action Loop
Short term – every thirty seconds
1. Balance of the boat
2. Trim of the sails, re-wind and waves
3. Compass heading, lift or headed

Medium term – every two minutes
1. Boats around us – are they lifted or headed and are they in more or less wind (pressure)?
2. How will 1. affect us?
3. Wind on the water?
4. Position with respect to the fleet and the laylines

Long term – every three or four minutes
1. Are we following our pre-start strategy? If *no*, why not?
2. Signs that the strategy should change and its implications. Clouds, other fleets on the course, big gains on one side of the course, indicators on the shore, smoke and so on.

decreased in size, I believe that this team approach is now vital in ensuring good boat speed, with the correct tactical decisions. It also allows the race to have a structure which can be followed if we are to review the performance afterwards (the game plan). Some people will say that this evaluation takes some of the fun away from dinghy sailing. I would argue the opposite because by careful identification of weak areas we can resolve them and actually have *more* fun as our skill level will be increasing. As for which school of thought suits you, only you will be able to decide. No one style is the correct way for all dinghy sailors.

THE FUTURE

A new development which may have an impact in learning more about dinghy sailing is the use of computers. I think that dinghy racing is very experience-related, and to acquire that experience may take many years. On the other hand, it is this experience and specific boat layouts, which do not put a high premium on physical fitness, that allow us to enjoy competitive dinghy sailing at every level for many years. The most famous example is Paul Elvestrom, who competed in the Seoul Olympics in the Tornado class. He had already won four gold medals between 1948 and 1960 and finished fourth in the 1984 Olympics sailing with his daughter Trine.

The computer programmes that are now available will allow you to develop this experience without finding a fleet of boats. You can develop tactical awareness, try strategies in tidal conditions or simply understand the rules. I have been experimenting with the Advanced Racing Simulator, developed by Posey Yacht Design in the USA (available through North Sails). I think that it is excellent for appreciating positions on the start and around the course while allowing a greater understanding of the rules – specific packages are also available for match racing. Who knows where the rapid expansion of computer technology will take us?

I suppose if I were trying to sell sailing to newcomers I would point to the fact that you are outside, competing against the elements and yourself. If you want to strive still further you can challenge more extreme elements or test your skills against larger, more competitive dinghy fleets. I believe that the new generation

121

of dinghies currently being developed in the mid-1990s will take the sport successfully into the next century. They are easy to sail, good value for money, exhilarating and simple to maintain; perfect for the lifestyles that are developing in this decade. I do not expect that the old classes will disappear overnight as they also represent excellent value for money and with large stocks of secondhand boats they will serve as the base for our sport, though in time they may be replaced. Whatever type of dinghy we sail, the exhilaration of making decisions to try to use the wind, the waves and ourselves to the best of our ability gives dinghy sailing a unique place amongst all sports. While the wind and waves remain free, I trust you will enjoy dinghy sailing and hope that this book may have contributed just a little to that enjoyment.

Glossary

Aft At or near the stern.
Astern Backwards or behind the boat.

Batten Thin strip of fibreglass used to support the mainsail leech.
Bear away Turn away from the wind.
Boom The spar along the foot of the mainsail.
Bow The front of the boat.

Centreboard Pivotting wooden or fibre-glass plate which pivots down below the boat to stop it sliding sideways.
Cleat Fitting which holds/grips sheets or control lines.

Daggerboard Simple type of centre-board which slides vertically, rather than pivotting.
Downwind Away from the wind.

Fairlead Fitting which guides a sheet or control line in the correct direction.
Foot Lower edge of the sail.

Gooseneck Fitting which allows the boom to be attached to the mast.
Gnav Upside-down kicking strap sys-tem, which pushes on the boom. (As used on Laser 4000.)
Gybing Turning the stern of the boat through the wind.

Halyard Wire or rope used to hoist a sail.
Harness Worn by the helm or crew to facilitate trapezing.
Head The top corner of the sail.
Head to wind Pointing directly into the wind.
Hiking Same as sitting out.
Hiking straps Same as toe straps.

Jib Small sail at the front of a two-sailed dinghy.

Kicking strap Purchase system used to control mainsail twist through boom position (vertical).

Leech The aft edge of the sail.
Luff Front edge of a sail or to turn the boat towards the wind.

Mainsail The large sail set on the mast.

Offwind Any direction away from the wind.
Outhaul System used to tension the foot of a sail.

Spars Generic term for mast, boom etc.

Tack Forward lower corner of a sail, or to turn the boat's bow through the wind.
Tiller Fits onto the rudder stock which allows the boat to be steered.
Tiller extension Extends the tiller to allow helm to sit out or trapeze.
Toe straps Webbing straps that allow helm or crew to sit out.

Trapeze System that allows a helm or crew to be supported outside the boat.

Vang Same as the kicking strap.

Windward The side of the boat towards the wind.

Useful Addresses

Australian Yachting Federation
Locked Bag 806
Post Office Milson's Point
NSW 2061
Australia

Canadian Yachting Association
1600 James Naismith Drive
Ontario K1B 5N4
Canada

International Yacht Racing Union (IYRU)
27 Broadwall
Waterloo
London
SE1 9PL

Irish Sailing Association
3 Park Road
Dun Laoghaire
Co. Dublin
Ireland

New Zealand Yachting Federation
PO Box 90 900
Auckland Mail Centre
Auckland
New Zealand

Royal Yachting Association (RYA)
RYA House
Romsey Road
Eastleigh
Hampshire
SO50 9YA

Singapore Yachting Association
c/o Hiang Kie Pte Ltd
52 Genting Lane #04–05
Hiang Kie Complex 1
Singapore 1334

US Sailing
PO Box 209
Newport
RI 02840
United States of America

Concept 2 Limited
151–153 Nottingham Road
Old Basford
Nottingham
NG6 0FU

Rowing machines

Laser Centre
6 Riverside
Banbury
Oxfordshire
OX16 8TL

Builders of the Laser and Dart range

LDC Racing Sailboats
232 Hither Green Lane
London
SE13 6RT

Builders of the RS range

Minorca Sailing Holidays Ltd
58, Kew Road
Richmond
Surrey
TW9 2PQ

Sailing holidays

North Sails
Newgate Lane
Fareham
PO14 1BP

Agents for Posey Yacht Design sailing softwear

Topper International Ltd
Kingsnorth Technology Park
Wotton Road
Ashford
Kent
TN23 6LN

Builders of the Topper, Iso and Hurricane range

Index